WOKING BUSES
1911–1939

LAURIE JAMES

AMBERLEY

First published 2012

Amberley Publishing
The Hill, Stroud
Gloucestershire, GL5 4EP

www.amberley-books.com

British Library Cataloguing in Publication Data.
A catalogue record for this book is available from the British Library.

ISBN 978 1 4456 0829 7

Typeset in 10pt on 12pt Sabon.
Typesetting and Origination by Amberley Publishing.
Printed in the UK.

Contents

Acknowledgements   5

Preface   7

Introduction   9

F. W. Mills   12

Guildford & District Motor Services   19

Aldershot & District up to 1930   22

R. Bullman & Son and A. C. Silk   32

F. W. Renshaw & L. M. Leam   34

Woking Autocar   42

W. Eggleton & Son   44

J. R. Fox & Sons   47

A. H. Stilwell and H. E. S. Trigg   60

Interlude – The Men from the Council   62

P. R. Burton, H. Settle & B. H. Martin   69

A. G. Smith   75

London General, East Surrey and Green Line   79

W. S. Hunt   91

J. Denyer   93

Thames Valley   95

J. F. Hampton   97

C. Ross & Sons   99

W. J. Bulman & Son   101

S. Spooner   104

S. Tanner   106

A. T. Locke & Son   110

H. T. Lintott   118

Aldershot & District 1931–39   122

London Transport   133

Bibliography   143

Appendix: Vehicles of Local Operators   144

Acknowledgements

The idea of a book on Woking's bus services was formulated by the author and his then work colleague George Burnett in the 1990s, after the publication of their *Tillingbourne Bus Story*. Pressure of work meant that George was unable to continue with the project and other commitments meant that the author was only able to progress slowly with research.

Inevitably, there are few people still around with first-hand knowledge of the matters in this book. However, the key that unlocked much of the early history of motor bus services in the Woking area was the laborious and painstaking transcription in the Surrey History Centre of the Minutes of Woking Council's Highways Committee and Omnibus Sub-Committee. Therefore, were it not for the work of Alan Lambert and Peter Trevaskis, you would be about to read a very slim volume as those Minutes are probably the main surviving documentary source material relating to the activities of the smaller bus operators prior to 1931. Their contribution cannot be overstated. I am very much indebted to Peter and Alan for allowing me access to their transcriptions and I am honoured that they thought I could be trusted to attempt to interpret them in a book. Peter has also assisted with early press cuttings and the loaning of old Aldershot & District (A & D) publicity material, rescued years ago from the offices at Aldershot, to prevent it going on the bonfire.

So many other people have helped in various ways. A & D's principal historian, the late Dr Peter Holmes, made available summaries of A & D Board Minutes, route records and press references. John Gaff, Chairman of the Aldershot & District Bus Interest Group, facilitated access to the material held by Peter Holmes before it was entrusted to the Group's archive. Mike Stephens is another A & D expert who read the manuscript along with Peter Trevaskis, as well as being the Omnibus Society's South Eastern Area Route Recorder , who was able to shed some light on certain points.

Among others who have contributed in different ways and measures are, in no particular order, Lavinia Truett (W. S. Hunt's daughter), Paul Lacey (a leading expert on Thames Valley), David Gray of the PSV Circle (records of vehicles owned by the 'independent' operators), Les Stitson and the late David Ruddom of the London Omnibus Traction Society, Malcolm Lambley (whose father worked for Locke's Blue Saloon) and Les Bowerman of the Send & Ripley History Society.

I also acknowledge the assistance of the Surrey History Centre (for access to contemporary issues on microfilm of the *Surrey Advertiser* and *Woking News & Mail* newspapers and various local directories), the Census 1911 website, Martin Kingsnorth, of the Omnibus Society's London Library at Acton, librarian at the Omnibus Society's main library and the timetable collection at Ironbridge, and before that at Ladbroke Grove. Tickets have come from the collections of David Seddon and Les Smith, to whom I am grateful.

A number of published sources have been consulted and are listed within the Bibliography. I am indebted to all the authors, compilers and publishers.

As might be expected, photographs of Woking's buses between 1911 and 1939 are not exactly in plentiful supply. Nevertheless, for the supply of illustrations I am grateful to Alan Cross, Alan Lambert, Eric Nixon, Peter Holmes, Les Smith, Andy Jones, Mike Stephens, Malcolm Lambley, Peter Trevaskis, Paul Lacey, Les Stitson, David Ruddom, Iain Wakeford and London Transport Museum. Some of the illustrations were not credited on the reverse when I obtained them, so they have been attributed to the collection of the person who supplied it. The rights of Joe Higham's photographs are held by Alan Cross and are reproduced with permission.

My gratitude goes to Amberley Books, who agreed to publish this. Finally and by no means least, my love and thanks to my wife Michaela for her document management and spreadsheet skills; also to Megan and Matthew for allowing me to be unsociable when engaged in research or writing.

There are now very few people who would be able to clarify or challenge much of the information herein. Frustratingly, some questions will remain unanswered. Any error of interpretation or fact or any omission is mine alone and for that I apologise.

Laurie James, Walton on Thames, 2012

Preface

It was not until the 1850s that the town of Woking really started to develop. Before then there were just a few hamlets and farms with a railway station sited in the middle of nowhere on a large expanse of heath-land known as Woking Common. Once the latter became available for building purposes there was rapid growth, with Woking becoming a thriving commercial centre. Since then there have been two phases of significant town centre redevelopment, and also residential expansion outwards, joining up with satellite communities such as Horsell, St Johns, Knaphill, Old Woking and Maybury. Major housing developments occurred in the 1950s at Sheerwater and in the 1980s on the site of plant nurseries at Goldsworth Park.

Woking is noted for diverse reasons, such as the birth of organised Muslim worship in Britain, the McLaren motor racing team and for having the first legal crematorium in Britain. H. G. Wells lived on Maybury Road, where he wrote *War of the Worlds*, using Horsell Common as the site of the first Martian landing. Today we are reminded of his story by an impressive metal Martian fighting-machine sculpture in the town centre.

Turning to our subject, the Motor Bus did not come to Woking until 1911, despite an earlier local initiative. Unlike many other areas, the town was not subsumed into the network of the major territorial operators for a considerable time. It was on the extreme fringe of the empires of Aldershot & District (A & D) and London General, who both had much to divert their attentions in their homelands. The First World War imposed major restraints on manpower and vehicles, and there followed a period of financial difficulties linked to an economic downturn. It was not until the mid-1920s that A& D was able to anchor itself firmly in Woking, while London General had to wait until 1931; both did so largely by acquisition.

Being on the boundary of two major operators who were providing little meant that the Woking area (and Guildford too) became ripe for exploitation by local proprietors. Men were returning from the Forces after the war with their demobilisation gratuities. Employment prospects were uncertain and they had new driving and engineering skills gained in military service. A fourteen-seat bus on a lightweight American chassis was relatively cheap, so the cost of market entry was not prohibitive. It was, however, a cut-throat business with numerous proprietors competing on the most lucrative routes almost on a dog-eat-dog basis. One councillor described the Woking–St Johns-Knaphill route as a 'little goldmine', making competition fierce and surely against the public interest in terms of providing a regular, reliable service. Timetables were frequently abandoned and vehicles on occasion were running more as taxis than as buses. Woking Urban District

Council struggled to exercise control over motor omnibuses between 1911 and 1931, using the powers at their disposal, often with a sense of great frustration.

The history of A & D and London General has already been documented, but little of any depth has been written about the so-called 'independents'. This book sets out to remedy this and to put the activities of the larger companies into local context. The book concerns itself with the period before the Second World War, up to the time of the disappearance of the last of the independent operators. Firms are included on the basis of having run bus services in the Woking Council area and are featured in approximate chronological order of the date of introduction of their first bus service in the district.

Woking's physical and social history has been extensively recorded and it is hoped that this book will add a further dimension to what has been published already on local public transport. In comparison with today's Woking, with its Arriva, Countryliner and Abellio Surrey buses, largely supported by Surrey County Council, we look back to an era when running any sort of bus was usually quite lucrative and for the small proprietor in a competitive environment, not an occupation for the faint-hearted.

The Aldershot and District Traction Company, Ltd.

NOTICE.

The following Motor Omnibus Service will be resumed on and after

FRIDAY, JUNE 1st, 1923,

between :—

GUILDFORD, WOKING AND KNAPHILL

via Stoke, Westfield, Woking Village and Woking Station,

and will run as follows :—

SERVICE 34.

This Time Table is issued subject to the Conditions and Regulations as printed in the Company's Time Tables and in Notices issued from time to time.

LIST OF FARES.

Stage No.														
1														Guildford Technical Institute.
2	2													Stoke Church.
3	3	2												Stoke Bell Inn.
4	4	2	2											Stoke Hill Schools.
5	4	2	2	2										Stringers Common Pillar Box.
6	6	4	3	3	2									Marrow Turning.
7	8	5	5	4	2									Mayford Arms.
8	9	7	6	5	3	2								Westfield Schools.
9	10	8	7	6	4	2	2							Old Woking, "The Green."
10	1/-	10	9	8	6	4	3	2						Woking Station.
11	1/1	11	10	10	9	7	5	4	2					Kingsway, Osman's Stores.
12	1/2	1/-	1/-	11	11	9	7	6	5	3	2			St. John's Post Office.
13	1/3	1/1	1/1	1/-	11	10	8	7	6	4	3	2		Inkerman Barracks.
14	1/5	1/3	1/2	1/2	1/1	1/1	11	10	9	8	6	5	3	2	Knaphill, Garibaldi.

Halimote Road,
Aldershot,
    23rd May, 1923.

By Order,
    E. G. HAWKINS,
    Traffic Manager

Wm. May & Co., Ltd., Printers, Aldershot.—44,764.

Introduction

In relative terms, the town of Woking as we understand it today is a fairly modern addition to the Surrey landscape, being very much a product of the coming of the railway. Situated on a geological zone known as the Bagshot Sands, it is twenty-five miles south-west of London, six miles north of the county town of Guildford, and has reasonably good road links to some of the surrounding towns. A major strength for a long time has been its excellent rail service to London and elsewhere, enabling commuters to be a significant part of Woking's current population of more than 91,000.

At the time of the Domesday Book in 1086, the heath-lands in north-west Surrey were noted as being extremely sparsely populated. The Woking area was part of a royal forest that was good for hunting, thus the area had connections with the Monarchy. The mother of Henry VIII developed Woking Palace in Old Woking and he often stayed there, as did Thomas Wolsey. A network of trackways crossed Woking Heath, the principal one being the Guildford to Chertsey road that bisected the future railway line at the site of the station.

The road system, such as it was, was not conducive to effective transport of goods, and between 1791 and 1794 the Basingstoke Canal was opened, joining the town to the Wey Navigation near New Haw. It was never very successful commercially, and the opening of the railway had a dramatic negative impact on its fortunes, ultimately leading to its abandonment.

What was to become the main line of the London & South Western Railway was first mooted in 1830 to link London with Surrey, north-east Hampshire including Basingstoke, then on to Winchester and Southampton, as well as the West Country. A large part of it in Surrey was constructed across heath-land, avoiding most opposition and reducing compensation costs. Through the future town centre area, much of it was on an embankment. The main station entrance was on the south side of the line, highlighting that there was very little to serve on the north side, where the commercial centre of Woking later grew up. Trains started running from London to Woking on 24 May 1838 and extended westwards in September that year. Horse-drawn stagecoaches from Portsmouth then transferred their passengers for London to a train at Woking.

With the railway in place and so much vacant and unproductive land, Woking was ripe for development. However, this was not immediate, partly due to the legal costs for enclosing Common Land. By 1854, the biggest thing to hit Woking since the railway was the opening of Brookwood Cemetery.

London churchyards were largely full, so legislation required cemeteries to be established outside of the capital. With good rail communications and much undeveloped land, the Woking area was ideal. The London Necropolis Company bought a huge area of land and started its cemetery at Brookwood. Much of the land around Woking station originally reserved for the cemetery was subsequently released for other purposes. Other land sold off in the Knaphill area was used for Brookwood Mental Hospital and for prisons – the site of the latter became Inkerman Barracks in the 1890s.

From 1884 Dr Gottlieb Leitner established a centre for oriental studies, as well as a museum of oriental art, and went on to build the Shah Jehan Mosque in 1889, the first in the United Kingdom, thus laying some foundation for today's noted multicultural society in Woking. In January 1895 Woking got its first comprehensive local government, namely Woking Urban District Council. This took over from various Highways and Sanitary Boards.

This preamble is merely intended to set the scene for the reader; those wishing to learn more about all aspects of Woking's past are referred to the numerous books available on the subject, including Iain Wakeford's *Woking Town Centre: an Illustrated History*, which has been most helpful.

By 1903 plans were being discussed in connection with having a tramway linking Woking with St Johns and a light railway from Woking to Bagshot via Chobham and Windlesham. There was optimism that the syndicate promoting the scheme would have the requisite capital to support a Provisional Order in the next Parliamentary session. Powers were obtained by the West Surrey Light Railways Co. and in 1905 there was talk of building an electric tramway from Woking to Guildford and Bagshot, opening up an area felt to offer excellent development opportunities. The Light Railway Co. also envisaged supplying power for lighting Chobham, Sunningdale, Bagshot and other

PG 1758, a Thornycroft BC, was probably photographed when new in July 1929 and about to enter J. R. Fox & Sons' Woking & District fleet. (*R. Marshall Collection/East Pennine Transport Group*)

A London General B-type single-decker as allocated to service 79 in the early 1920s, but seen before the route with that number was extended beyond Esher. (*Omnibus Society*)

communities. A Light Railway Order was granted by the Board of Trade in April 1906, but no work was ever undertaken. Already, a cheaper and more flexible public transport scheme was being put forward – the Motor Bus.

By February 1906 several prominent Woking residents had become doubtful that the tramway or light railway would reach fruition. They felt that if better communication were needed they would have to provide it themselves with the Motor Bus. This view was also held at the Guildford end of the proposed tramway. The Woking & District Motor Bus Co. Ltd was registered on 26 April 1906 to run buses from Woking to Knaphill, Chobham, Send and Ripley, among other places. The Manager was Henry Quartermaine – a prominent figure in the town, being a councillor and businessman. As a councillor, he would later play a leading role in trying to regulate the activities of local bus operators. A prospectus was issued giving details of plans to acquire three motor buses, the development of which was in its infancy. Had they succeeded, the shape of bus provision in Woking may have been different. However, the company did not attract sufficient capital and was dissolved on 6 July 1906. The name 'Woking & District' was to reappear in the 1920s under a different guise.

Woking had to make do with a few small-scale and inadequate horse bus operations until Frank Mills arrived on the scene in 1911 and the first somewhat rudimentary motor bus service got underway.

F. W. Mills

The Local Motor Bus Pioneer

It was probable that it was late in 1911 that Frank William Mills and his family moved to St Johns, occupying a residence that came to be called Daphne House on the junction of Robin Hood Road, Hermitage Road and Barrack Path. He was born in Stourford, Worcestershire in 1870, his wife was Amelia of a similar age and they had seven children – Olive (seventeen), Ruby (sixteen), Milly (thirteen), Frank Jr (nine), Doris (eight), Cyril (four) and Dorothy (two). In line with his trade, he was to establish a motor engineering business at adjoining premises, known as St Johns Garage. Subsequently he also operated from Hermitage Road Garage (Mills' Motor Works) a short distance away, adjacent to the entrance to Inkerman Barracks.

Described as being 'small in stature but large in vision', he conducted his affairs in a robust and pragmatic manner. Effectively that meant that he appeared to have scant regard for rules, regulations and bureaucracy. Despite the mobility he brought to the civilian and military population, he became a thorn in the side of Woking Council's Highways Committee, the local police and the hackney cab trade.

The Woking area was not particularly well served by traditional horse-drawn Carriers services, not having the appeal or needs for the movement of goods as pertained in the market towns. As well as Brown at Send and Gibbs at Chobham (described later) who definitely carried passengers too, by 1911 there was Alfred Hill of Old Woking running thence to Woking, Mayford, Send and Guildford as well as Bernard Buckman of Broadway, Knaphill, running to Guildford five days a week. Buckman moved to 64 High Street, Old Woking, seemingly taking over from Hill, while Joseph Tullett maintained the Knaphill–Guildford trips by 1913. These ventures were soon to end.

The Woking Council meeting of 14 November 1911 considered an application from Mills, then of Brighton Road, Godalming, for a licence to run a motor bus from St Johns to Woking. These were still early days for motor buses and there were concerns about safety, and mention of several steep gradients on the proposed route. It was opined that the weight of the vehicle would create additional wear and tear on the roads, which could cost the ratepayer a considerable amount to rectify. One councillor thought that the War Office might allow the bus to run through Inkerman Barracks, thus reducing the effect on the public highway. The matter was referred to the Highways Committee and soon after, Frank Mills started his service. The vehicle was an open-top double-decker seating thirty-six, of unknown manufacture and registered P 5413.

Mr J. Elliott had been licensed to run a horse bus on the same route but by February 1914 he had been replaced by F. W. Renshaw, who withdrew in the face of Mills' competitive motorised offering. However, Renshaw will be encountered again later.

In January 1912 Mills' bus was slightly damaged in an accident, so he ran another vehicle for a few days, possibly a hackney cab. From 29 January the service was suspended for five days, after which it was extended from Woking Station to Maybury Arch for a short time. Changing his timetable on a frequent basis or not adhering to it at all became Mills' trademarks. Indeed, non-compliance with timetables by large and small operators until 1931 was a constant aggravation for the council. When the council considered renewal of the licence for Mills' bus in June 1912 they had already received complaints, leading to Mills submitting a timetable, stating that he only deviated from it in exceptional circumstances. He only accepted private hire bookings between scheduled services or on Wednesdays, when the bus route did not run. He hoped to acquire a second, smaller bus so he could also offer a morning service on the route. In terms of what services would be available to the public, Mills was somewhat economical with the truth and his regular pledge to the council to comply with the timetable held little water.

Mills was a member of the St Johns Division of the fire brigade and in November 1912 was charged with dangerous driving. Apparently he drove the fire appliance to an alleged speed of 35–40 mph, when the limit was 10 mph, when responding to a Test Call in the town centre. In his defence he said that he did not slow down as he had not seen a policeman and would have done so if he had. He was fined thirty-two shillings costs – this was reimbursed by the councillors who had a private collection; no doubt they thought that a public servant had been unfairly treated in the circumstances.

In 1913, the *Daily Mirror* published a story concerning Milly Mills, one of Frank's daughters – 'a dark-eyed girl of 15' who had been working as a conductress on the bus for about a year. It was very unusual at that time for a girl to be so employed, although it became more widespread during the First World War. Apparently, 'she thoroughly enjoyed her job' and did not issue tickets, but merely collected the money. Her father was quoted as saying 'she knows as much about the bus engine as I do. When I take the bus out in the morning she has prepared it for service and I can always depend on it being in perfect working order.'

After a seemingly uneventful 1913, Mills applied in February 1914 for a licence for a second bus, allowing the St Johns service to be extended to Knaphill, and for a new service between Woking and Send via Kingfield Green and Old Woking. Mills advised that he was acquiring a new 35 hp Dennis chassis on which to mount the body from his existing bus, and also introduced a single-deck vehicle with seating for up to twenty people being quoted. Although Mills had mentioned the possibility of running to Ripley, this does not seem to have occurred. Some people objected to Mills' activities but a letter in the local newspaper from 'A Workman of Old Woking' expressed the opinion

that buses are much-needed for cheap local travel and should not be objected to because of wear and tear on the roads. Buses could prevent young people from leaving rural areas as they would be able to reach town for amusement or educational purposes.

Above left: The Mills family home was Daphne Cottage on the corner of Hermitage Road and Robin Hood Road in St Johns. Some of the Mills clan pose adjacent to two cars, possibly used as taxis. In the background at the garage can be seen the double-deck bus registered P5413. (*Iain Wakeford Collection*)

Above right: This is quite likely to be Frank Mills' daughter Milly, well-known locally at the time for her key role in assisting with her father's business. She is standing on the rear steps of the solid-tyred, open-top double-deck bus used to initiate the first motor bus service in the Woking area. (*Iain Wakeford Collection*)

Prior to this, Mr Sidney J. Brown of Waveney, Send, had licences for two horse-drawn buses to run between Send (Mays Corner) and Woking, starting around 1911. Before him, the proprietor of the Carrier's service from Ripley and Send was Ernest Cox, who was preceded by Charles Stephen Cox. The latter was listed as a bus and fly proprietor in 1907 and 1909, running to Woking four times a day. The Horse Bus also offered a parcel delivery service, and grocery orders were collected from the International Stores in Woking. Despite Mills' service, Brown continued operating, the vehicles being described as an eight-seat enclosed horse bus and a wagonette. By 1918 the wagonette was no longer licensed, but the other vehicle had its licence annually renewed until July 1925, some time after motor bus services through Send became properly established.

A timetable dated 9 March 1914 for Mills' 'Knaphill, Woking and Send Motor Bus' nominally showed four round trips on each route, Mondays to Saturdays, and advertised a parcel delivery service. It is probable that there was still no timetabled service on Wednesdays, apart from one round trip in the evening. The fare from St Johns to Woking was 2*d*, as it was from Woking to Old Woking. In the absence of any other service, Mills' buses were popular and by May 1914 the council was warning him not to overload his vehicles. He replied saying that the bus had seats for thirty-six, was capable of carrying five tons independent of the weight of the body, and that it had never been dangerously overloaded, which no doubt was a matter of opinion.

However, world events were about to significantly change life for many in Woking and severely constrain any bus operator from introducing new or enhanced services. When German troops entered Belgium on 4 August 1914, Britain kept its pledge to offer support and declared war on Germany. Thousands of men answered the call to join the army but it was soon clear that the war was not going to be over by Christmas.

This meant that far more men were stationed at the Inkerman Barracks in St Johns and at Bisley Camp. By October 1914, complaints about overcrowding of buses were such that Frank Mills reassured the council that he was as concerned about that as they

Frank Mills' second bus (P5585) was a Dennis with about twenty seats, known for obvious reasons as the 'sloping bus'. The number of men in uniform suggests that this photograph was taken during wartime. (*Alan Lambert Collection*)

were, but it was impossible to stop intending passengers from boarding. He wanted to buy another bus, but there were none on the market; he obtained a third one – a small Ford – by September 1915. The war had caused a shortage of manpower and on 4 May 1916 one of Mills' small buses was involved in an accident while being driven by a Ralph Moss, who was unlicensed. Licensed drivers Gowler and Davis had left without warning to join the army, so he could either take the bus off the road or use Moss. Milly Mills had also driven people from St Johns to Woking station. Other unlicensed taxi and hackney carriage drivers were used, to minimise inconvenience to the public. The following month Mills applied to license a seven-seat Ford, described as a wagonette, while Moss and a man in military uniform were noted driving. The council wrote to Mills reminding him of the need to obey the law in its various forms and that he might be liable to prosecution or having all his licences revoked.

By January 1916, the Send service had ceased so all resources could be concentrated where demand was greatest. Subsequently Mills applied for a driving licence for daughter Milly but one was granted only for small vehicles, as it was 'outside of the power of a girl to manage a big bus'. The numbers of soldiers travelling largely precluded local people from getting a ride. Frequently, Mills' vehicles ran direct from Woking station to Bisley Camp, not carrying civilians. Stipulated vehicle capacities were ignored as soldiers stormed onto the buses, there being little that Milly Mills could do to prevent them, even though it is said that she was no shrinking violet when it came to helping her father run his business. In July 1916 there were outrageous incidences of up to twelve soldiers riding on a bus roof and six inside in excess of the seating capacity in a small Ford. The council again threatened to revoke licences, but these were exceptional times and a public outcry would have ensued. They were also concerned about the speed at which the buses were driven, no doubt to obtain the maximum number of trips possible with each vehicle.

Although A & D served Knaphill and Woking for a short period up to December 1916, at times they were unreliable, placing further pressure on Mills' service. By November 1916, Mills was advertising his motor works in St Johns as Ford repairers and as sole Surrey agent for Maxwell cars. 'Ladies taught driving and lady drivers supplied'. In line with national feeling he used the words 'no eligible [for war service] men at Mills'.

Mills had apparently stopped running publicly available morning buses to town from Knaphill and St Johns when A & D had extended their Brookwood service to Woking on 14 August 1916. In April 1917 it was noted that Mills did not publish a timetable, but ran a continuous service from 2 p.m. to 10 p.m. as required. Curiously, the fare on a 'large bus' was 3d and 4d on a smaller vehicle. By May 1917 Mills had gained a new competitor on the St Johns–Woking route in the shape of R. Bullman & Son, followed in August of that year by the reappearance of F. W. Renshaw.

In March 1918 a Mills bus on a late evening journey, driven by Lily Horne, had a collision with a taxi in Goldsworth Road. Taxi driver J. F. Stimpson was charged with dangerous driving. The impact of the collision had spun the bus around, resulting apparently in the unfortunate Ms. Horne being thrown out of the vehicle, which sustained a bent radiator and broken axle. Conveniently, Frank Mills' eldest daughter – Olive – was a witness as she was in another taxi at the scene of the accident. After due consideration the Bench dismissed the case, perhaps concluding that there was an element of blame on both parties.

The Woking taxi proprietors lodged a complaint in May 1918 that Mills had been using his small vehicles to tout for custom along the Station Rank, before transferring the captive customers to the larger bus back to St Johns. This was denied by Mills and the Borough Surveyor was to undertake observations.

Meanwhile, in addition to acquiring several more small Ford buses, Mills had bought a Singer vehicle (at least that's how it was described in the council records, although visually it looked suspiciously like another Ford Model T) by November 1918, followed by a ten-seat Albion early in 1919. The war had finally ended on 11 November 1918 when the Armistice was signed, although it was to be some time before normal life resumed, including bus service development and better availability of manpower and fuel.

In 1919 Frank Mills was nominated as an Independent councillor for the St Johns ward, although he withdrew from the contest before polling day. The issue may have been clouded by an accident involving a car that he was driving. He apparently knocked down and injured a young soldier who was stationed at Pirbright Camp. When the case came to court in 1920, damages of £1,500 were awarded against Mills, which probably had a direct impact on his personal finances and business affairs.

By autumn 1918 the activities of those operating on the St Johns to Woking route were such that Woking Council realised that it had its first real bus war on its hands – a portent of what was to come in various parts of town. The Surveyor had received a letter of complaint regarding the irregular and uncertain service provided and in an attempt to secure a regular

Outside of Mills' premises in Hermitage Road are Fords PA 7717, PA 7163 and CD 2597, which all have canvas bags on the roof to store gas for propulsion, when petrol was rationed during the 1914–18 war. On the right one can just see an open charabanc. (*Iain Wakeford Collection*)

Brasier CT 351 first appeared in Woking in the ownership of Frank Mills by 1919. By September 1920 it was licensed to a V. Jenner but in June 1921 was included in an auction of equipment owned by the bankrupt Mills. (*G. Robbins Collection/Alan Cross*)

thirty-minute-interval service, they were summoned to the Highways Committee meeting in June 1919. The Bullmans and Renshaw complained that Mills would transfer passengers from his bus at the front of the Stand onto another vehicle – even a car – so that the original bus would remain at the head of the queue of vehicles. Also, Mills would park four buses on the Stand early in the morning to be washed and cleaned under the supervision of his daughter, thus preventing any of the other operators getting a share of the traffic until mid-afternoon. A member of the public had complained that Mills had stopped his bus in the middle of the road and enticed passengers out of the vehicles of others.

Frank Mills strongly denied all of this. He explained that some of the vehicles were operating on special contracts and that his drivers were instructed to depart after no more than ten minutes, even if they only had one passenger. At the Stand, only brass-work was cleaned. On no occasion were people asked to get out of other firms' buses, but the majority of people preferred his drivers so his buses filled up first. Mills undertook to remove to the rear of the Stand any vehicle from which passengers had been transferred to another. The Committee suggested that quarrels were set aside in order to work harmoniously together. Mills was granted licence renewals for six buses – two Fords, a Brasier, a Singer, an Albion and a Daimler charabanc. There is no further reference in Highways Committee minutes to Mills vehicles being granted licences subsequent to June 1919.

Advertisements for Mills' Garage in the local press disappeared after February 1920. There is no mention therein of any bus service activity by that time. However, Woking Council granted a licence to Mr V. B. Jenner of 6 Hermitage Road, St Johns in September 1920. This was for Mills' Brasier bus registered CT 351, to run between Woking and St Johns. It is unclear how and if Jenner relates to Mills in some way; it is possible that this bus did not actually become Jenner's property, being run by him under some arrangement with Mills.

There was an auction at Mills' Garage on 8 June 1921 that included buildings, a Ford 'racing car', a Renault van, a Belsize landaulette and the Brasier bus. Also to be auctioned was the milliner's shop in Hermitage Road run by Milly and Olive Mills since at least 1919. These events seem to have been triggered by Mills' bankruptcy; Stephen Silk, a builder from Church Hill, Horsell, secured a number of items and was said to be Mills' largest creditor.

The 1921 Woking Yearbook gives Frank Mills' name against St Johns Poultry Farm, next to the Crematorium, as well as against the entries for Daphne House and the two garages. The 1923 edition makes no reference to F. W. Mills but lists Misses Mills, Dressmakers, Hermitage Road and they seem to have continued their business until the early 1930s. Daphne House and St Johns Garage had passed to E. Pudney, Haulage Contractor. The directory for 1924 shows Hermitage Road Garage as 'vacant', but by the 1927 edition, Mills is shown once again as occupier of this property. In February 1923, Frank had applied for a bus driver's licence, perhaps working for another local operator until he was able to reestablish his garage business. The last reference to Mills' name against Hermitage Road Garage in a directory is in the 1932/3 edition of Kelly's and it is possible that thereafter the Mills family left Woking.

The site of Mills Motor Works in Hermitage Road is now where Wickes builder's merchants is situated, while Daphne House (named after Mills' daughter Ruby Daphne) is a veterinary surgery, known more recently as the Daphne Cottage Surgery.

The Aldershot & District Traction Co., Ltd.

NOTICE

WOKING, HORSELL & LOWER KNAPHILL SERVICE

On and after **SATURDAY, JANUARY 8th, 1927**, this Service of Omnibuses will be revised and run as follows until further notice :—

SERVICE 41.   WEEKDAYS.

Timetable for Service 41 — Woking Station, Horsell War Memorial, Horsell Cricketers Inn, Little Wick, Royal Oak Lower Knaphill (and return), with Weekday and Sunday departures. Fares stage numbers: 1 Woking Station; 2 Wheatsheaf Bridge; 2 1 Church Road Corner; 2 2 1 Horsell War Memorial; 3 3 2 1 Horsell Cricketers Inn; 4 4 3 2 1 Little Wick; 4 4 3 3 2 1 LowerKnaphill (Royal Oak).

‡ The 10.20 p.m. Omnibus will wait at **Grand Theatre, Woking**, for the conclusion of last performance.

Cheap Day Return Fare between WOKING STATION and LOWER KNAPHILL
RETURN FARE - - - 6d.

This Time Table is issued subject to the Conditions and Regulations as printed in the Company's Time Tables and in notices issued from time to time.

HALIMOTE ROAD,   By Order,
     ALDERSHOT,   E. G. HAWKINS,
January 3rd, 1927.   Traffic Manager.

Clement & Son, Printers, Aldershot. 19464.

Guildford & District Motor Services

A False Start

The 23 January 1914 meeting of Guildford Town Council's Watch Committee considered applications for additional omnibus licences to be used for several services radiating from that town. The licences were sought by both the Aldershot & District Traction Co. Ltd, which was already affiliated to the British Automobile Traction Co. Ltd (BAT), and by Guildford & District Motor Services Ltd The latter firm represented a pooling of interests by Dennis Bros, vehicle manufacturers, and Walter Flexman French – an omnibus pioneer who had already founded Maidstone & District Motor Services and was later to be involved with A & D, Southdown and Hants & Dorset, among other bus companies.

French was the son of an Essex dairy farmer and after developing engineering experience, which included railway locomotives, he started manufacturing bicycles in Balham, south London. He was credited for operating the first petrol-engined ' wagonettes' on routes in London from 1899. Later he concentrated on the motor trade through his French's Garage and Motor Works Ltd, also in Balham and in 1904 became manager of the Sussex Motor Road Car Co. Ltd in Worthing. John Dennis was also involved in the cycle trade, but in Guildford. Having produced some motorised cycles and light cars, he and his brother Raymond moved on to commercial vehicles, including early buses. In 1905 they moved to a ten-acre site on the outskirts of Guildford near Woodbridge Hill. To meet increasing military and civilian production needs, this became a major manufacturing plant which was to supply many buses to A & D and the smaller firms for use in the Woking and Guildford area.

After some delay twelve licences were granted to Guildford & District, which prompted the firm to apply in late February 1914 to Woking Council as well, for six licences to enable commencement of a service linking that town to Guildford, Godalming and Chiddingfold, which never materialised in that form. Guildford & District was registered on 12 March as a limited liability company, having already taken delivery of its first bus chassis from Dennis Bros. It had an authorised capital of £15,000 and the original directors were Walter Flexman French and Ronald Inman. However, the British Automobile Traction Co. acquired a large proportion of the Guildford & District shares on 30 May. These shares were transferred by BAT to A & D nominees on 29 June as a prelude to Guildford & District becoming a wholly owned subsidiary of A & D on 15 December. Although its operating responsibilities formally transferred

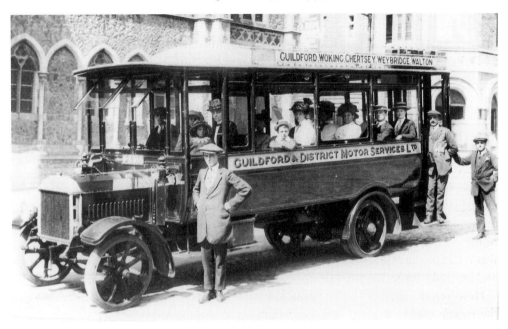

Guildford & District Motor Services started running in the Woking area on 30 May 1914. Dennis P5388 remained with Aldershot &District until after the war but Guildford & District activities in Woking only lasted until March 1915. (*R. Marshall Collection/East Pennine Transport Group*)

Another Dennis vehicle, which was used by the fledgling Guildford & District company to inaugurate the first long-distance bus service through Woking, that from Guildford to Walton on Thames. If on service, KT 2285 appears very popular, but stamina would have been required for a long journey on such a vehicle. (*Author's Collection*)

to the parent company on 11 December 1914, Guildford & District retained its separate identity and its buses in their separate livery continued to be used on A & D services out of Guildford. The company is known to have owned at least eight Dennis buses with single-deck bodywork, five of which were registered P 5388, LH 9020, LH 9026, KT 2285 and AA 5239, the latter transferred from the main A & D fleet.

The Guildford & District company had been used to start a new service on 30 May 1914 from Guildford to Walton on Thames via Stoke, Mayford, Woking, Byfleet, Addlestone, Chertsey and Weybridge. This reflected the Walter French influence in terms of bold, long distance territory-forming services. Two hours were allowed for the whole journey, which must have been quite a feat of endurance for bus crews and passengers, bearing in mind the indirect nature of the route, the state of the roads and the low speeds at which buses were obliged to run, as well as the uncertain robustness of the solid-tyre vehicles. Compared to the local nature of Frank Mills' activities, this was a route of significant proportions in terms of the number of towns joined together and key links forged.

However, the usual wartime difficulties made this a somewhat short-lived venture as the service was withdrawn after 10 March 1915 and did not reappear as such. Some of the Guildford & District vehicles had been requisitioned for military service and the three that remained (P 5388 and LH 9020/6) were added to A & D's own resources, along with the company's office premises at 198 High Street, Guildford. The company then remained dormant until it was wound up on 29 October 1926.

The company office was at 198 High Street in Guildford. The building is seen here after being transferred to Aldershot & District; the latter used the upper floor as an inspector's residence. Note the advertisements proclaiming 'charabancs for hire'. (*Peter Holmes Collection*)

Aldershot & District up to 1930

A Love/Hate Relationship with Woking Council

The overall history of A & D has been admirably covered already in Peter Holmes's excellent book entitled *Aldershot's Buses*. However, as the company was slowly to become the most significant operator in the Woking area, at least on three sides of the town, it may be useful to start this commentary by giving some abbreviated background to set the scene and to put A & D's activities in Woking into context.

On 1 June 1906 the Aldershot & Farnborough Motor Omnibus Co. Ltd commenced a service between those towns using two Milnes-Daimler open-topped double-deck vehicles. A leading influence in the company was Thomas Matheson (Tom) Foster, then aged twenty-six and one of the directors, who had a flair for motor engineering as well as commercial acumen. His father William Foster was the instigator of the company and would later become chairman. Services were then commenced to Ash, North Camp, Deepcut and Farnham. Premises were obtained in 1908 on Halimote Road, Aldershot that were subsequently expanded to become a principal garage, workshops and head office for A & D.

Additional capital was needed to expand the company. This resulted in control being obtained from 16 August 1912 by the British Automobile Traction Co. Ltd (BAT), a subsidiary of the British Electric Traction Co. Ltd and the formation of the Aldershot & District Traction Co. Ltd. A vehicle livery of dark green, light green and white was chosen; with changes to the shades and proportions and the use of cream instead of white, these colours were adopted by A & D for its vehicles for the rest of its existence. Additional services acted as territorial markers but after the outbreak of the First World War passenger-carrying activities were much reduced, except for the Aldershot–Farnborough route. Some vehicles and staff resources were engaged in goods transport activities for the Army, Aldershot being a strategic military town.

As the War proceeded, the availability of vehicles increased somewhat, allowing some new A & D services to be developed. In January 1916 a service was opened from Guildford to Knaphill via Stoughton, Worplesdon, Fox Corner, Pirbright and Brookwood, but on 1 March that year it was curtailed at Brookwood. This was once again extended to Knaphill from 5 August and on to Woking station via St Johns, over Frank Mills' territory. However, the enforced exodus of many of A & D's staff due to the National Emergency, as the company described the war situation, meant that several services had to be suspended on 15 December 1916, that to Woking included.

While the Woking service was suspended, A & D continued to apply to the council to renew their licences in order to protect their position. The twelve vehicles licensed there in June 1918 included various Daimler, Belsize and Dennis single-deckers, including two of the latter originally in the Guildford & District fleet (LH 9020/9026). With the war finally over, A & D were able to reinstate several services and on 7 June 1919 it was the turn of the Guildford–Brookwood–Woking service, which was designated as M in their new service identification regime. There were four journeys each way on Mondays to Saturdays and two on Sunday afternoons. This was followed by the new service U from 20 December 1919, which ran from Guildford to Woking via Stoke, Mayford, Westfield and Kingfield Green and then on to St Johns and Knaphill to augment service M.

In April 1920 a limited number of journeys on service B (Aldershot–Deepcut Camp) were extended to Pirbright Camp, Brookwood, Knaphill, St Johns and Woking, but a full service between Woking and Aldershot did not start until 29 November 1920, when service B was numbered 4. At that time service M was numbered 28, but service U was withdrawn in October 1920 and was to be followed by the loss of service 4 from the Woking area in April 1921. As can be seen, A & D was still not operating on a stable footing as a programme of economy was having to be pursued, resulting in a reduction in staffing, although some consideration was given in March 1921 to restoring the Guildford–Mayford–Woking service. This was considered again in February 1923 together with the reinstatement of the old Guildford & District service to Weybridge and Walton on Thames, although it was noted that serving Walton previously did not produce good financial results.

The company's inability to anchor itself properly in the Woking area, which it regarded as fairly peripheral to its sphere of operations, made it possible for various small local proprietors to become established, notably on the Knaphill–St Johns–Woking corridor. However, A & D did restore service U from 1 June 1923, but this time numbered 34. This was extended from Knaphill to Bisley, West End, Lightwater and Bagshot on 1 March 1924, although one source quotes 18 February. This established what was to become an important strategic trunk route that still survives, with some variation, in the present-day network of Arriva. Also on 1 March 1924, service 28 was diverted between St Johns and Woking via Star Hill. In that month, A & D were offered the chance of purchasing the former Mills garage at St Johns to house some of their buses; this was declined and services 28 and 34 continued to be worked from Guildford. In mid-1924 A & D was running thirteen journeys each way between Knaphill and Woking on its two services.

After a fairly uneventful period of nearly two years, the number of journeys on service 34 was increased from seven to sixteen per day, making it hourly from 25 February 1926. At the same time it was extended from Bagshot to Camberley and Yorktown. This did not amuse the local proprietors, nor the council, who were not consulted on the new timetable in advance of its introduction. The council had expended much effort in encouraging the various operators running between Woking and Knaphill to coordinate their activities, and now A & D had 'upset the arrangements made and caused endless confusion'. As soon as A & D increased the service, Fox's Woking & District ignored the timetable on their Woking–Bagshot service and ran a few minutes in front of A & D. To make matters worse, the council had just incurred considerable expense in having a comprehensive local bus timetable printed which was now out of date. A & D replied

Photographs of early vehicles on Aldershot & District services to Woking have proven hard to locate but here is AA 5166, a Daimler CC new in August 1913 with bodywork by Brush. Such a bus could possibly have performed on the company's first services to Woking. (*Alan Lambert Collection*)

This is a Dennis Subsidy type, dating from autumn 1919. The driver on the left is W. Cripps of Guildford. This view was captured before December 1923, when a new body by Strachan & Brown was fitted. (*Mike Stephens Collection*)

Aldershot & District PH 1106 was a 1927 Dennis 4-tonner with Strachan & Brown thirty-six-seat rear-entrance bodywork. This was the bus belatedly sold to London General Country Services in December 1932 as part of the deal to transfer Maybury service 47. Having been inherited by London Transport, it is seen outside Amersham garage. (*J. Higham Collection/Alan Cross*)

that they were unaware of the timetable and offered to pay for a reprint. Their chairman attended before the Highways Committee to personally apologise. The company tried, allegedly, to reach a working agreement with Fox but the latter would not co-operate, thus inflaming the 'war' on the Bagshot route. Up to this point it may have been that Woking Council was relatively happy with A & D's activities, it being a professional, well-run bus operator of some substance when compared with the piratical in-fighting of the local firms and owner-drivers. However, they must have felt that A & D was now riding roughshod over matters they considered in their control and there were subsequent suggestions of bias towards locally based firms, despite their vagaries.

A & D was keen to expand its operations locally in the Woking area and from 9 June 1926 came to terms with Arthur Smith of Knaphill to acquire his Blue Omnibus business, including a service to Blackdown Camp, (given number 28B), three vehicles and garage premises in Anchor Hill, Knaphill; this became A & D's local base.

By 1 August 1926 the council had brokered a coordinated timetable on the Woking–Knaphill route involving A & D, Woking & District, Renshaw & Leam and Mr Hampton. In theory this was to offer a ten-minute-interval service. From that date A & D service 28 was diverted between St Johns and Brookwood to operate via Brookwood Lye Road, to omit Knaphill, while service 34 was extended from Yorktown to Blackwater (hourly) with alternate journeys on to Hawley. Service 4 (Woking–Aldershot) was at last reinstated on 27 September 1926 and on the same date a service 34A variant of the 34 was introduced, whereby the journeys that terminated at Yorktown were extended to run to Frimley and Blackdown Camp. To round off the year, A & D acquired the rights to Stephen Spooner's service from Woking to Lower Knaphill (Royal Oak) from 15 December (numbered 41), although A & D actually started running at 1.30 p.m. three days later. Following the destruction of Spooner's bus by fire and after a replacement taxi had met with an accident, the service had been covered by J. Hampton, who stopped running on 22 December.

Information on vehicles operated by A & D is given in a Fleet History of the company produced by the PSV Circle. Without going into detail here regarding the individual buses allocated to routes serving Woking, it should be mentioned that between 1922 and 1926 various types of single-decker were delivered to the company, including the Daimler Y-type (thirty-two/thirty-four seats), Dennis four-ton (thirty-six seats), Dennis 50 cwt (thirty seats) and Dennis 30 cwt (eighteen seats). All these were of the 'normal control' layout, that is driver behind the engine, with the most prolific body builders being Arnold & Comben and Strachan & Brown, with some by Dennis themselves. From 1927 the 'forward control' (driver alongside engine) Dennis E-type was introduced (thirty-two or thirty-five seats), being allocated to Woking area services from around January 1928. The Dennis G was a new normal control model with eighteen seats. Supplementing these for varying periods were the various assorted small buses taken over from the operators that had been acquired, some of which were retained and painted into A & D livery.

Despite attempts at coordination by the council there were complaints (often from Woking & District) that A & D was still not running according to its authorised timetables during 1927 and was running quite a few additional journeys. For example, on Saturday nights at around 10 p.m., A & D was said to have as many as seven buses plying for trade at Woking Station.

In 1929, A&D used a large number of new Dennis E type vehicles to replace antiquated buses in their fleet. D245 (OU 1094) was sold as soon as November 1936 to a new owner in Worthing, ending up as a showman's living van. Here it is at Guildford station on service 28 to Woking via Brookwood. (*Mike Stephens Collection*)

Woking Council received notification from A & D in December 1927 that the company sought to introduce services from Woking to Ottershaw, Chertsey, Addlestone and Weybridge, to Byfleet and Weybridge and to Guildford via Old Woking and Send. However, these plans were somewhat overtaken by the purchase of Clifford Ross's business on 13 January 1928, with four vehicles and two services, these being numbered 47 from Woking to Maybury Inn and 48 to Chertsey via Six Cross Roads, Bleak House and Ottershaw. Subsequently, A & D asked the council to effectively forget, for the time being, the routes to Weybridge and Guildford via Send. In hindsight it appears that the applications were possibly designed to encourage Ross off the road and to keep up the pressure on Woking & District. The new 48 service also ran beyond Woking to Kingfield Green, Westfield, Mayford and Guildford, which resulted in a half-hourly service in conjunction with the 34.

A & D proposed to divert service 28 so that it operated between Woking and Brookwood via Horsell, Littlewick Road and Knaphill. The only conflict with other bus companies was the 200 yards section of road between the Anchor Hotel and Knaphill Post Office. To confuse matters they also sought to extend service 41 from the Royal Oak to Knaphill Post Office. This was permitted on the proviso that the terminus was at Wades Dairy. Objections had come from Woking & District, Renshaw & Leam and Hampton who felt that the proposal was contrary to the July 1926 agreement and suggested that service 41 not be allowed beyond Barley Mow Lane. The council and A & D asked whether it was reasonable for Horsell people to be obliged to walk up the hill to Knaphill from the Royal Oak or be denied a direct link to Guildford. Without waiting for a resolution, A & D went ahead on 25 January 1928, when they diverted hourly service 28, introduced additional short workings between Woking and Knaphill as 28B and withdrew service 41. Retrospectively they gave the opinion that their action was in the public interest and that they had sought to avoid conflict by entering Woking on a route where there were no other operators, namely Littlewick and Horsell. Despite their seemingly cavalier attitude, one can understand A & D's frustration that their attempts to plan their services in a cohesive way on a network basis were receiving interference from a local authority intent on protecting existing arrangements, even if relating only to a very short section of a much longer strategic route. The use of the 28B number meant that the original 28B journeys to Blackdown were renumbered 4A as they were effectively short-workings of service 4.

Bertram Martin of Bus de Ville complained in February 1928 that due to late-running of A & D buses on service 47, they were often clashing with the times of his own service to Maybury, Byfleet and Chertsey. A & D used a small single-decker with a driver/conductor and by the time he had collected the fares and issued tickets it was often up to five minutes beyond scheduled time when he was ready to set off. A warning on this practice was issued by the council, to which A & D responded that Bus de Ville were frequently late as well.

In a quest to reach Windsor, A & D proposed two new services thence from Aldershot and Guildford (numbered 50 and 51 respectively) which would start on 23 March 1928. Between Ascot and Windsor they would have run through the territory of the Thames Valley Traction Co. Despite common ownership connections, Thames Valley objected strongly, leading to discussions on a boundary agreement. There was a competitive response from Stanley Tanner of Chobham, who proposed a new service that would have paralleled the 51 between Sunningdale and Guildford. Woking Council refused to grant permission for the part of service 51 within its area, as a result of which A & D cancelled its planned introduction, blaming Woking Council but in reality because they had upset their territorial neighbour.

In April 1928 A & D showed their continuing interest in running a service from Woking to Weybridge by applying for an hourly facility via Bleak House, Ottershaw and Addlestone. The proposed times would clash with Bus de Ville between Woking and Maybury Arch and Bertram Martin lodged his objection, saying, 'I consider additional services absolutely unnecessary. Let those who made these routes in the first place derive the benefits to which they are entitled.' Once again a local problem prevented strategic network growth.

A & D had been developing some express coach services from various parts of its territory to London. Several were regarded as experimental, with one or two journeys each day to test the market, and some were short-lived. In that category was one from Knaphill, St Johns, Woking and Ottershaw. Started on 26 May 1928, it was enlarged from 11 June to serve also Worplesdon, Pirbright and Brookwood. It did not last long (possibly until December 1928) as the limited travel choice it offered and the need to book in advance was no match for the very frequent service of trains. Commencing from 8 July 1928 were a number of express coach services to coastal destinations during the summer season. They ran from Worplesdon, Pirbright, Brookwood, Knaphill, St Johns, Woking and Mayford, initially to Portsmouth & Southsea but also to Brighton and Bognor Regis from 7 August that year. By then, A & D had established a booking office at 1 Goldsworth Road, Woking.

In September 1928 A & D reached agreement with the next local operator they wished to acquire. This was Stanley Tanner's Chobham-based business, which was acquired on 8 October, together with three vehicles and the use of his premises. His service between Woking and Chobham (Burrow Hill) was numbered 55, while the journeys which extended to Valley End, Windlesham and Sunningdale Station were numbered 55A. From 13 October 1928 to 3 February 1929 the number 34B was used for extra journeys over the route of service 34 between Woking and Bagshot. The number was reactivated from 25 March 1929, when J. F. Hampton's journeys between Woking and Knaphill (Garibaldi) via St Johns were acquired, together with four vehicles which were not used by A & D.

In June 1929 A & D tried again for their Weybridge service, making sure that this time their hourly workings did not clash with Bus de Ville between Woking and Maybury Arch. The application was referred to the Through Omnibus Services Joint Advisory Committee with a recommendation for approval. In July Woking & District applied for a service from Guildford and Woking to Ottershaw, Chertsey and Windsor. A & D maintained that as they had purchased the Ross service between Woking and Chertsey, they now had preferential rights on that route and that licences should not be granted to other companies. The Highways Committee responded by saying no operator was entitled to a monopoly on a particular route and granted Woking & District's application, despite the Joint Committee having recommended refusal. The A & D management, including Tom Foster, attending the meeting were not best pleased with this outcome and threatened to 'flood the streets of Woking with buses' and to run just in front of every Woking & District bus on every route.

A & D then advised that they would start an extra hourly service between Woking and Chertsey on 16 August 1929 via Chertsey Road, Bleak House and Ottershaw, which they duly did, numbered 48B, as well as commencing their Weybridge service (48A) on 19 August. They also parked buses right outside the council offices, to depart just in front of Woking & District buses, as well as revising the timetables of the Chobham services without approval from the Joint Committee. The 55 was diverted via Mincing Lane in Chobham and 55A was diverted via The Windmill public house on the A30, north of Windlesham, instead of serving Snow's Ride. In addition a new service 55B paralleled the 55A from Woking to Windlesham and then proceeded to Bagshot, Camberley and Yorktown, heightening competition with Woking & District. The 55/55A/55B combined to provide a bus every thirty minutes between Woking and Chobham.

Following these acts of aggression, A & D were warned to suspend service 48B immediately or the licences would not be renewed for any of their buses on 8 October. The council's view was that they had the jurisdiction over services in Woking, not a large bus company. The message worked and A & D signed an agreement and withdrew service 48B on 2 October 1929. In contrast to this controversy, the extension of service 34 from Hawley to Cove on 12 July that year was not really an issue in Woking.

On 21 January 1929, A & D took possession of some premises in Walton Road, Woking, rented from Mr Pitcher, for use as a garage, as their requirements for keeping vehicles in the town had outstripped the capacity of the former Smith garage at Knaphill. It was located next to the Billiard and Dance Hall on the corner of Marlborough Road. As early as May 1927 it had been recorded that the Knaphill garage was not in a good state of repair, and

An old postcard view showing a small Dennis of Aldershot & District climbing from Addlestone towards Ottershaw on service 48A sometime after August 1929. Although the bus is not featured in close-up, the picture is interesting as the bus and car would today probably be somewhere in the middle of the M25: Church Road was re-aligned when the motorway was constructed. (*Peter Holmes Collection*)

The Dennis EV registered OU 1115 at least had Woking as a destination in this posed view, probably taken when new in May 1929. Sold in February 1937, this bus also became a showman's fairground living van. (*Alan Lambert Collection*)

Another Dennis EV, Aldershot & District D284 (OU 1806), in the fleet from June 1929 to November 1937; this or similar buses would no doubt have been seen regularly in Woking. (*Mike Stephens Collection*)

a year later an agreement was reached to buy some land from the Anglo-American Oil Co. in Goldsworth Road for £3,650, which would be used for a new purpose-built bus garage. Once the Walton Road garage was opened, the A & D Board decided in March 1929 to dispose of the Knaphill site and eventually it was sold for £325 around March 1930. The Walton Road premises also allowed the Chobham outstation to close during 1930.

In 1929 Guildford Corporation circulated a draft of an Undertaking which operators would have to sign when applying for licences. In essence, operators could not deviate from what they subscribed to at the time the application was made and they would be bound by the approved timetables. A & D refused to sign and suggested several changes, the main one being that they were unable to agree to bind themselves not to alter timetables except in a minor way or in an emergency. There were occasions when it was necessary to completely revise a timetable in order to make connections with trains, other company's services, or their own services. No doubt the council felt this was just a way of adjusting timetables so as to get in front of competitors' services.

At the time of this dispute, A & D were trying to develop their short service 47 from Woking to Maybury Inn, which they had acquired from Clifford Ross. Back in October 1928 they gained approval from Woking Council to extend it from Maybury Inn to Guildford, through Old Woking, Send and Burpham. They intended to start the extension on 24 June 1929, engaged drivers and conductors, and printed timetables. However, the Guildford Watch Committee would not approve it, to A & D's great frustration. This, combined with being unable to reach agreement on the proposed Undertaking, prompted A & D to remind the town clerk that they had spared no effort to keep buses running during the war and that they should be spared unrestricted competition on routes they had run for some years. Now, when operations became chaotic (due to others), the Watch Committee tried to restrict and control the company's business. The town clerk replied that the service 47 extension application could be expedited if they signed the document. A & D then started the 47 extension on 17 July, numbering the remaining short journeys between Woking and Maybury Inn as 47A. A thirty-minute-interval service was provided from Woking to Maybury Inn and hourly beyond. On Sundays, only the short 47A operated, until 18 August from when the 47 ran through to Guildford hourly during the afternoon and evening. Following this action, the Watch Committee refused to grant any licences to A & D; although A & D appealed to the Ministry of Transport, they ultimately signed the Undertaking and sent it back on 2 August!

There was a further development in September 1929 when A. T. Locke and Son, who ran a service between Guildford and Send, applied to extend it onwards to Old Woking, Kingfield Green and Woking. Despite objections from other operators, this was granted. With Locke and Woking & District running through Send, as well as East Surrey's service 31 terminating there, A & D withdrew 'temporarily' the hard-won Guildford extension of service 47 from 6 November 1929, with that number being reapplied to the residual service between Woking and Maybury Inn.

Meanwhile, in Guildford the Safeguard firm, owned by the Newman family, was locked in bitter competition with A & D on their local services in the town. As they started these services originally, they felt aggrieved over A & D's predatory tactics, and perhaps sensing the Watch Committee's concerns over the attitude of A & D, they applied for various services to places already covered by the larger company. Arthur Newman intimated that the late Chief Constable of Guildford encouraged him to apply for new services in order to make up for the loss of income he had been experiencing due to the competition. One of the applications was a blatant attack on A & D's key service 34 from Guildford to Woking, as three Safeguard buses per hour were planned to run over the same route. This approach produced results, as Safeguard reached an agreement with A & D over who should run what on the local services; therefore the proposal for a Woking route was not taken forward.

A & D's parent company BAT had become part-owned by Thomas Tilling Ltd, another major bus-company-owning holding company. In May 1928 the two had amalgamated to become Tilling & British Automobile Traction Ltd (TBAT). Having been given powers to run their own bus services, the four principal railway companies decided instead to buy a major shareholding in existing bus companies. The Southern Railway chose to equal TBAT's one-third interest in A & D, and by an agreement of 1 January 1930 the transaction was confirmed and two extra board members were appointed by the Southern Railway. Just before then, in November 1929 the London General Omnibus Co. had proposed that they purchase some of A & D's operations in the Woking and Guildford areas. No response was to be given until the new railway company directors joined the Board, but nothing further transpired. Around the same time A & D was approached by Conway West Ltd of Woking to ascertain whether A & D would be interested in buying their coach business, but the reply was in the negative.

Since 1 October 1929 a combined fifteen-minute-interval 28/28B service had been run between Woking and Horsell. This turned out to be over-provision for the traffic on offer and was reduced to a half-hourly service exactly a year later. On 28 May 1930 service 55B (Woking–Yorktown) was truncated at Bagshot.

During 1930 plans were submitted for the new bus garage in Goldsworth Road, Woking. It was to accommodate thirty-three vehicles and capital expenditure up to £8,000 was authorised by the board. A tender to build it for £7,047 was accepted from Bunning & Fitton Adams Ltd, while the lease on the Walton Road garage was extended for another twelve months. In September, A & D asked the council to consider allowing the use of double-deck vehicles on services 34/34A and 48, as they would reduce the need for passengers to stand and for duplication of popular journeys, thus reducing congestion in the streets. The surveyor had concerns over the suitability of certain roads, vibration of houses in residential districts caused by heavier buses, and the ability of Bunkers Bridge on service 48 to take the weight. A resident of St Johns complained that double-deckers would destroy privacy, while the National Citizens Association repeated the various concerns and added potential damage to trees for good measure.

Negotiations were opened in July 1930 with Jim Fox to purchase his Woking & District business, and by October a figure was agreed. An approach was made to London General to see whether they would participate, as due to the geographical nature of the services to be acquired and the Area Agreement with General, future joint operation of services was not desirable. With the new licensing provisions of the Road Traffic Act 1930 expected to come into force the following year, it would have been seen as essential by A & D to remove Fox from the picture as soon as possible, and the outcome is described in the second part of the A & D Woking story.

R. Bullman & Son and A. C. Silk

Featuring a Bus Ownership Dispute

Mention has already been made of competition for Frank Mills from Bullman's bus service, for it was at the March 1917 meeting of the Highways Committee that an application was received from R. Bullman & Son of Apsley House, St Johns Hill Road, St Johns for a licence for a small motor bus. This was to be granted if approved by the Surveyor. The 11 May 1917 edition of the *Woking News & Mail* carried an advertisement for their new service from St Johns (Kiln Bridge) into Woking, along St Johns Road and Goldsworth Road. This ran every two hours in the morning and 'frequently' through the afternoon and evening. On Sundays it ran in the afternoon only.

The Bullman family (as opposed to the Bulmans from Hook Heath, to be encountered later) arrived in St Johns in 1912, having come from Dunsfold via Maidenhead and Bayswater in London. Robert Bullman took over a taxi business and in 1913 was listed as Motor Jobmaster at 4 Gordon Villas, St Johns Road. The first bus was a small Ford, registered PA 6943, which was initially licensed to Mrs L Bullman. A second Ford registered PA 7621 had arrived by June 1918. Cars and buses were advertised from the Apsley Garage in St Johns.

Robert Bullman's son Reginald served in France at the age of seventeen, and after leaving the army in 1919 came to work for his father. When Reginald got married, his father passed control of the business to him but he apparently mismanaged it. About May 1921, Reginald Bullman bought the ten-seat Albion 15 hp bus registered BH 2927 from Stephen Silk, the builder from Horsell who had purchased it from the defunct Mills business. Bullman bought it with a hire purchase agreement but defaulted on payments, being badly in debt by the end of 1921. Apparently he soon after wanted to exchange the bus for a taxi but actually sold the vehicle for £110 to H. J. Hallam, a motor dealer in London, in May 1922. The bus was noted as being off the road by January 1922 and it is probable that by that time the St Johns bus service had ceased. To mask his deception, Bullman asked the unwitting Silk in September 1922 if he could exchange the bus for a landaulette, available from Ryan's Garage at Clapham, and seems to have obtained permission to do so. Suspicions were raised when the bus could not be located at Clapham.

Bullman was charged that, having defaulted on payments, he stole a bus worth £350(!) from Stephen Silk around June 1922 and Reginald, now twenty-three years old, appeared in a special police court in March 1923 while on remand. He was bound over

The Bullmans used this Ford T (PA 6943) on their service between St Johns and Woking from 1917 until probably about 1921. It is pictured at the London & South Western Railway's Orphanage, later known as Southern Railway's Woking Homes. (*Alan Lambert Collection*)

for twelve months in the sum of £20 but was spared a custodial sentence. Silk eventually seems to have got the Albion back, as it was used in due course by his son. By 1923 Apsley House had no resident listed but it still stands in St Johns.

The saga of the contentious Albion continued in November 1923, when Arthur Cecil Silk of May Cottage (given in the Woking Directory as May Villa), Hermitage Road, Knaphill asked Woking Council for a licence to use it to ply for hire between Knaphill and Woking station. A positive response was given, subject to the bus being approved and a satisfactory timetable being submitted. In June 1924 Silk was running seven journeys from Knaphill to Woking from 9.20 a.m. to 9.45 p.m. and seven journeys in reverse from 10.15 a.m. to 10 p.m. The licence for the bus was renewed at that time, being the last mention of Silk in the council minutes, so he probably withdrew before the year had ended.

F. W. Renshaw & L. M. Leam

One of the First and Last Independents

The longest period of tenure among the small locally based motor bus operators was that of Renshaw & Leam from 1917 until 1939, although as already mentioned, Renshaw had previously been a horse bus proprietor on the St Johns to Woking route. Various branches of the Renshaw family were in business in the area; John Charles Renshaw at St Johns Dairy, Arthur James Renshaw at Kingsway Farm Dairy and Francis William Renshaw, butcher of Hermitage Road, St Johns. The name Aubry & Renshaw also appears, possibly coincidentally, in 1923 when, as building contractors, they were erecting a pair of steel-framed, concrete-clad cottages at St Johns. This was novel technology at that time. John Renshaw was also a Woking councillor, who interestingly spoke in defence of the small local bus proprietors when they were being castigated in the council chamber for some alleged petty misdemeanour or being threatened by the powerful A & D.

At the time of the 1911 Census, Francis (Frank) Renshaw, born in 1883, was unmarried, the rest of his household consisting of three young men employed as 'workers', presumably in the butchery business. At that time, a Miss Lily Maria Leam, aged twenty-six, was living at Barrack Path, St Johns and was listed as the manageress of a butcher's shop, most likely Renshaw's at Oxford House, St Johns.

Renshaw's horse bus service probably ceased some time before July 1915. However, he embraced the internal combustion engine by running taxi cabs and it was noted in June 1920 that he had not fitted meters to his cabs, which led to complaints from other drivers. The first reference to Renshaw as a motor bus operator was in August 1917 when a small Ford vehicle, registered PA 7746, was granted a licence. This was used on the Woking–St Johns–Knaphill route. Frank Renshaw had other business interests – nurseries at St Johns Lye, and farming at Halebourne Farm at Chobham, which was possibly an adjunct to the butchering activities.

In December 1917 a bus driver's licence was granted to Lily Leam who, as previously mentioned, was associated with Renshaw. In June 1919 a Ford bus (PA 8365) was licensed to her for use on the St Johns route. One can speculate whether her name was being used at that time purely as a matter of convenience. In early October 1921 Renshaw & Leam were advertising their operations as the Grey Bus Service, and an excursion to Guildford for the market was being run on Tuesdays from Woking station via Horsell and Knaphill. On 17 December 1921 Grey Bus Service started a new daily route from Woking to Hook Heath via Star Hill. Renshaw gained a licence for another Ford Model T in November 1922 – this was registered P 8180 and was not new. By then he was quoted as having a garage at Church Road, St Johns.

Woking Council's surveyor discovered in June 1924 that Grey Bus had not run to a timetable for the previous two years, which highlighted the approach sometimes taken by the small firms as part of their competitive tactics. However, they now produced a timetable that showed that they would make about a dozen round trips each day. By that time a new Chevrolet fourteen-seat bus (PD 9889) had arrived to replace the somewhat antiquated Ford P 8180, while Miss Leam licensed another Ford (PE 2415) in April 1925. By September that year the licence applications suggested that Renshaw's two buses were for use on the Woking to Knaphill service, while Miss Leam's two were for use on the Woking–Hook Heath service, which had been extended to the main Bagshot Road. However, Woking Council was only willing to grant one licence per person, although Miss Leam could have a second licence but only in substitution. Renshaw unsuccessfully argued for an extra licence, as he had been assisting Arthur Smith after most of the latter's buses were destroyed in a depot fire, but was finally granted it in January 1926. In reality it is fairly certain that both Renshaw's and Leam's vehicles operated on a shared basis.

The council's hackney carriage inspector noted that there had been a decided improvement in terms of the operators adhering to their timetables, with the exception of Renshaw. He sometimes failed to run his Knaphill journeys until the evening, when the service apparently paid better. If Miss Leam's bus had been hired by a private party, Renshaw covered the Hook Heath service and consequently the Knaphill service did not run. The vehicle licensing argument continued, as Miss Leam had never produced her second bus for inspection, thus the licence for its 'standby' use had not been issued. On 18 January 1926 Miss Leam wrote indignantly to the council, stating,

> I am in receipt of your letter regarding the complaints about my bus. As it is the first time I have heard of these complaints I think it will be better to have the matter cleared up and I ask permission to attend the next meeting of the Highways Committee. It has never been my wish to go against laws laid down by the Council or give unnecessary trouble, but I do demand justice and not to be punished before I know what I am being punished for.

The Chairman of the Committee considered that there was no useful purpose in her attending the next meeting, in view of her recent activities. It had been observed that she had been running an irregular service between Woking and Knaphill as well as unlicensed journeys to Pirbright, Deepcut and Blackdown Camps from Brookwood station, in connection with military personnel returning to their barracks, having arrived by train. For good measure, a driver by the name of Brixton had attempted to charge double for a journey from Woking to Hook Heath.

Although not exactly blameless of similar activities, Messrs Fox (Woking & District) wrote to the ouncil, complaining that for several Sundays Renshaw & Leam had been running their buses from Brookwood station to the Camps and that instead of running the Hook Heath service, used those buses on the Knaphill route just in front of a Woking & District vehicle.

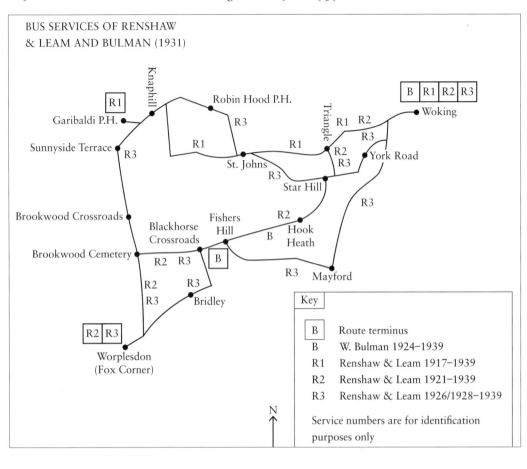

BUS SERVICES OF RENSHAW
& LEAM AND BULMAN (1931)

Key

B	Route terminus
B	W. Bulman 1924–1939
R1	Renshaw & Leam 1917–1939
R2	Renshaw & Leam 1921–1939
R3	Renshaw & Leam 1926/1928–1939

Service numbers are for identification
purposes only

I have reported to the Inspector several times and I know he has told them about it and they absolutely ignore him and apart from this, disorganise the service and cause friction between the drivers. On Monday they finished at 12.30 p.m. and brought the bus out again at 7.20 p.m. and went to the station and waited until 8.15 p.m. – missing a journey. If the Highways Committee allows this sort of thing, the other drivers will ignore what the Inspector tells them. These proprietors do not know how to run a bus service and are simply playing with and ignoring the Highways Committee.

Consequently, Frank and Lily were summoned to the Committee on 26 February 1926. Miss Leam undertook to run all services in the future according to approved timetables, if licences were renewed, which they were for four buses and for a fifth as a spare vehicle, providing they were produced for inspection. She confirmed that she and Frank Renshaw were operating as one firm – hardly surprising as she was his partner in more than the business sense.

In July 1926 an application was made for a service from Woking to Fox Corner via Mount Hermon Road, Star Hill, Hook Heath, Fishers Hill and Worplesdon Hill or via Mayford, Saunders Lane, Fishers Hill and Bridley. A somewhat improvised timetable was submitted which was 'quite impossible to understand'. Objections came forth from A & D and from Walter Bulman, who had been competing with Renshaw & Leam on the Hook Heath service since early 1924. The National Citizens Union sent a twenty-five-signature petition, protesting a bus running along well-heeled Mount Hermon Road. The council suggested that all journeys should take the Mayford route in order to avoid Mount Hermon Road and further clashes with Bulman. Renshaw & Leam accepted this, but had not started the service by early December, although probably did so soon afterwards.

The engine of their Ford PE 2415 caught fire at Woking station on 30 November 1926. Fortunately the wind was not blowing strongly as there was no fire extinguisher on the bus. The passengers were evacuated through the rear emergency exit, but according to driver Brixton, no damage was done. An A & D driver put out the flames with the

P 8180, Renshaw & Leam's third Ford Model T, was typical of the somewhat home-made appearance of bodywork on vehicles used by small operators around the country in the early 1920s. First licensed by Woking Council in November 1922, it appears to be outside Woking station. Note the Grey Bus Services timetable on the side panel. (*G. Robbins Collection/Alan Cross*)

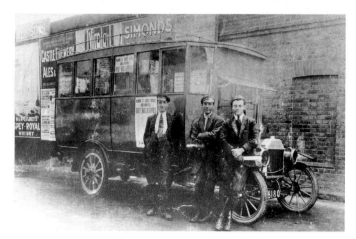

extinguisher from his vehicle. This led the council to insist that all buses carried two such pieces of equipment. By that time the Renshaw & Leam fleet contained two new Chevrolets (PE 8584 and PF 2824) in lieu of Ford PA 8365 and Chevrolet PD 9889.

Renshaw & Leam were in trouble again in April 1927 when they were caught duplicating their 8.30 a.m. journey from Knaphill to Woking. Apparently this was in retaliation for J. R. Fox's Woking & District operating their 8.20 a.m. journey late and abstracting Renshaw's passengers. This sparked further tit-for-tat protests from Renshaw & Leam and Woking & District about each other's buses not running on time. Later that year it was reported that the timetable for both the Hook Heath and Fox Corner via Mayford services had been altered without permission. Another new Chevrolet (PF 5771) replaced Ford PE 2415.

Some journeys on the Hook Heath service to Fishers Hill were formally extended to Worplesdon Hill/Bagshot Road around December 1927 and at some time subsequently onwards to Fox Corner. Renshaw & Leam had already tried in June 1927 to gain access to Guildford from Woking ,and Guildford Council was prepared to grant a temporary licence until 31 August if the intended vehicles were produced for inspection. A & D were not amused, but in the event, Renshaw's expansion plan was changed so as to run an hourly service from Bagshot to Guildford via Lightwater, West End, Bisley, Knaphill (Garibaldi P. H.), Brookwood Crossroads, Fox Corner and Worplesdon. Woking Council consulted Windlesham Urban District Council on the subject and felt that Renshaw & Leam would have to acquire additional buses. Renshaw agreed that the service should not start until such time as they arrived. Needless to say, it was not as simple as that. A & D strongly objected over potential abstraction of custom and a Henry Lintott had applied to Windlesham Council for a similar service. In speculative preparation, Renshaw & Leam took delivery of a twenty-seat, six-wheeled Chevrolet, registered PH 6898, in February 1928. However, the matter was further complicated by an application from Stanley Tanner of Chobham to also run over the section of route between Knaphill and Guildford. After extensive deliberation, Henry Lintott won the day, as described later. Renshaw wrote to Windlesham Council, surprised that his application had not been granted, especially as he lodged it before that of Lintott. He suggested that he had incurred wasted expenditure of £1,000 for new buses. The clerk advised Renshaw that if he had ordered buses and got into difficulties before the licences were granted, he only had himself to thank for it.

When Lintott later applied to Woking Council to pick up passengers in their area, Renshaw & Leam wrote, naturally somewhat aggrieved at the out-turn of events,

> we have been watching this case with interest and wondering what steps the Council would take against this proprietor. We would have thought that a summons would have been issued and the service discontinued in the meantime. Mr Lintott has been running this service and we felt that by applying to (Woking) Council for permission to run over the same route we lost the privilege of being granted this service by other Councils.

The council was not moved and one can only speculate on their clerk's conversation with his counterpart on Windlesham Council, in view of previous annoyances with Renshaw & Leam.

Also in December 1927, Renshaw & Leam proposed a new service on Mondays to Saturdays of seven journeys from Woking to Knaphill (junction of Bagshot Road/ Broadway at Sunnyside Terrace) via Star Hill, St Johns, Robin Hood Road and Lower Knaphill. This was granted in March 1928, despite objections from Woking & District and Mr Hampton, on the condition that it left Woking via Goldsworth Road and The Triangle. In late April 1928 Renshaw tried again to access Guildford via Worplesdon and Stoughton by extending his Woking to Fox Corner service. Guildford Council would not approve this, nor Renshaw's further attempt in 1929 for a Bagshot to Guildford service, on the grounds that his buses were not, in the view of the Chief Constable, fit to be licensed.

In March 1928, driver Redvers Kearse sued Renshaw in the Magistrate's Court for wages owed after he had been dismissed for poor timekeeping. Other staff at that time included Frederick Sadler (manager), Ernest Finch (mechanic) and drivers James McBride and Robert Francis.

In early July 1928 an application was received from P. Crouch & Son of Stoughton, Guildford, who wished to extend their Guildford to Worplesdon service to Woking via Goose Rye Common, Smart's Heath and Mayford. Although this was not granted it seems to have prompted Renshaw & Leam to ask to extend their Fox Corner via Mayford service to Smart's Heath, Goose Rye Common and Worplesdon (Perry Hill). This never proceeded and their request in December 1928 for extra journeys from Woking to Fox Corner was declined as the timings were almost identical to Bulman's. An increase in the Woking to Sunnyside Terrace service was refused on the basis that other existing services were adequate for public demand. Also, Woking Council continued to be concerned about the amount of complaints regarding irregularity of Renshaw & Leam's operations and in April 1929 would only re-license their vehicles if a satisfactory undertaking were received. However, an hourly Sunday service on the Sunnyside Terrace route was granted in September 1929, as was a service at times required by school children, with two journeys each way from St Johns to Mayford via Hook Heath, Fisher's Hill, Worplesdon Hill and Saunders Lane.

Renshaw & Leam's services often became disrupted if a vehicle was off the road, but an extra bus was obtained in January 1930 in the shape of PG 5551, a Dennis 30 cwt. with Strachan eighteen-seat bodywork. In November 1930 both Renshaw & Leam and Woking & District applied for services from Woking to Brookwood via Horsell and Knaphill but these were refused. However, Renshaw & Leam were eventually successful in gaining an improvement to the Sunnyside Terrace service in January 1931. This was linked to a scheme to join up this service with that from Woking to Fox Corner via Mayford, whereby buses would operate along Bagshot Road between Cemetery Gates and Sunnyside via Brookwood Crossroads, thus forming a circular route. Certain journeys operated via Worplesdon Golf Club instead of Bridley.

From 1 April 1931 only the licensing of taxi cabs – and other vehicles adapted to carry less than eight persons and hired as a whole – was undertaken by local authorities such as Woking Urban District Council. In relation to public service vehicles, parts of the Town Police Clauses Act were repealed and bus companies would apply to the new area traffic commissioner in order to license their services under the Road Traffic Act 1930. Woking was originally placed in the South-Eastern Traffic Area. The commissioners decided what services should run, at what level and by whom. When competing applications were received, they could hold a hearing in the traffic court, where operators could be legally represented to promote and protect their interests and could lodge objections to the plans of others. Having heard all the evidence, the commissioner would then make a ruling and Road Service Licences would be issued.

Until such time as the first hearings could be arranged, existing operators and their services were able to continue under transitory provisions. Sittings to hear applications got underway in the second half of 1931 and if operators could prove they ran an established service which was in the public interest and met a need, they generally received permission to continue. Due to often weighty objections in a formal courtroom setting, getting a new or extended service would be far more difficult for operators than when they dealt with local authorities. Public service vehicles had to undergo close scrutiny by a Ministry of Transport vehicle examiner (who were very thorough and often zealous in their work) to ensure they were fit for use under more stringent national criteria. For some small local operators like Renshaw & Leam, who were used to conducting their affairs in a robust manner, doing just enough to keep the council's bus inspector at bay, the new regulations and associated paperwork came as a culture shock and some left the industry promptly, being unwilling or unable to adjust or to pay the additional administration and vehicle maintenance costs.

However, Renshaw & Leam did decide to continue running under the new legislation, but service development was virtually at an end. They successfully gained licences for their services and, without the distraction of predatory competition against them, and by them against others, they settled down and maintained their operations reasonably satisfactorily. Between October 1931 and July 1933, Renshaw & Leam modernised their Grey Bus Service fleet with three new twenty-seat Bedford WLB vehicles. Eventually all the earlier vehicles were taken out of service except for Dennis PG 5551. Through the 1930s they continued their three daily routes, each requiring one bus. That from Woking to St Johns and Knaphill ran hourly, Woking to Hook Heath and Fox Corner ran at least once in each hour, while the circular route via St Johns and Knaphill to Fox Corner, returning via Mayford, ran every two hours clockwise and every two hours anticlockwise.

In April 1939, A & D came to terms with Frank and Lily and a £2,000 purchase price for the business was agreed. The takeover took effect on 10 May 1939, the same day that A & D also acquired Bulman's Hook Heath bus service. The four buses were included in the deal but were not used by A & D, being disposed of the following month. The Woking–Knaphill (Garibaldi P. H.) service was absorbed into A & D service 34B, Woking–Fox Corner via Hook Heath became 63 (also incorporating Bulman's service), and the Woking–Fox Corner via Mayford service became 64. Woking to Fox Corner via Star Hill, St Johns, Knaphill and Brookwood Crossroads was curtailed at Knaphill and numbered 44. This event was significant and marked the end of an era, with the disappearance of the last local independent operators. A & D and the Country Bus Department of London Transport reigned supreme in Woking. After this, Frank and Lily continued with the butcher's shop and plant nursery in St Johns until at least 1956.

The Grey Bus Services fleet was strengthened in January 1930 by the arrival of PG 5551, a new Dennis 30 cwt eighteen-seater. It is seen posed with the optimistic frontal destination display of Guildford but the ambition of Renshaw & Leam to reach that town was to be thwarted. (*Alan Lambert Collection*)

Typifying the Grey Bus Services fleet in its final years is Bedford WLB PJ 8068, with Duple twenty-seat bus bodywork – a type used by many small operators. Seen here by the canal bridge in the centre of St Johns, it was acquired with the business by Aldershot & District in May 1939. (*J. Higham Collection/ Alan Cross*)

Some tickets from The Grey Bus Service of Renshaw & Leam. (*Courtesy of Iain Wakeford*)

Woking Autocar

Early Days on the Chobham and Send Routes

In November 1912 Harvey Gibbs of High Street, Chobham applied for a licence for a horse-drawn bus with eight seats, to run between Chobham and Woking; this is quoted in contemporary directories as running four times a day. Since 1905 Gibbs had been listed as a farmer at Fowlers Wells, Chobham. Pre-dating Gibbs was Herbert Rose, the Chobham Carrier, running into Woking with a 'bus' of some sort from 1903 to about 1913/14. In addition, a horse bus operated by a horse trainer by name of Charles Croydon Atkins ran from at least 1907. In 1903 and 1905 Atkins was apparently a beer retailer and he had ceased running the bus by mid-1912. Subsequently, Atkins understood that Frederick Challiner (or Challoner) of The King's Head, Chobham was to start running, but Woking Council got no reply to their enquiry on his intentions. Gibbs' service had seemingly been reduced to two journeys a day by 1915 and licence renewal last appears in the council minutes for June 1916.

Meanwhile in October 1914, Fred Daborn of Windsor Road at Burrow Hill in Chobham applied for a licence that was granted, for a small motor bus that he intended to run on the same route. There is no further mention in the Minutes and some doubt over whether this service actually started. In the 1920s, Mr Daborn, described originally as a cycle agent , ran a garage with petrol sales in Station Road, Chobham.

In view of wartime fuel shortages, there had been experiments around the country with gas-powered vehicles, usually with a large unsightly canvas bag on the roof. Woking Autocar Co. Ltd, owned by J. A. Fry, was a Ford dealership with motor engineering works at 89–93 Chertsey Road, Woking since at least 1915. They were also advertising the supply of precision tools and gauges and tools for munitions workers. From 24 September 1917 they introduced a dual-fuel, left-hand-drive, twelve-seat Ford Model T bus (AB 3523) on two services radiating from Woking: to Chobham via Horsell and Mimbridge, and to Ripley via Old Woking and Send. The bus initially departed from Ripley at 9.30 a.m., 12.30 p.m. and 7 p.m. and from Chobham at 11 a.m., 4.30 p.m. and also 8 p.m. on Saturdays only. At a time when illustrations were rare in the local press, the *Woking News & Mail* seems to have recognised the novelty value of the bus and included a photograph in an article on its introduction, although Frank Mills also ran gas-powered vehicles.

The Woking Gas Co. was contracted to supply coal gas that was stored in a rubber-lined canvas bag on the roof of the Ford. The engine could be powered either by the gas (but started on petrol) or by petrol alone. In March 1918 the fares were one shilling from Woking to Ripley and *6d* from Woking to Chobham. By June of that year another Ford vehicle, registered PA 7553 appears to have been substituted – this was probably a conventional petrol-powered model.

Exactly how long this passenger-carrying adjunct of Woking Autocar's general activities lasted is unclear but it had certainly ceased before October 1919, when the business was sold to Capper Bros. Indeed, by August 1919, Ford PA 7553 was owned by William Eggleton, of which more follows. The premises in Chertsey Road were later occupied by Conway West and Pearce and Nicholls; today Brook House stands on the site.

As a postscript, in August 1922, the horse that used to pull the Chobham bus was owned by Captain Rowland Walker of Mimbridge Nursery. He had bought it in 1919, but whether direct from Mr Gibbs is not recorded. Walker was taken to court for allowing the horse to work when unfit.

Used to start operations to Chobham and Ripley in 1917, Woking Autocar's Ford T registered AB 3523 could run on both petrol and coal gas, hence the large inflated canvas bag on the roof. This picture was used on the company's promotional leaflet. (*Andy Jones Collection*)

W. Eggleton & Son

The Last Independent on the Chobham and Addlestone Routes

By 1911 William Eggleton, aged thirty-two and born in East Molesey, was a painter and decorator living with his wife Clara at 4 Wilsons Cottages, North Road, Woking. The earliest reference to Eggleton in the Minutes of Woking Council's Highways Committee, is in August 1919. Living by then at 57 Walton Road, Woking, where he ran a newsagent's shop, he applied to licence a small Ford bus registered PA 7553 that he had acquired from Woking Autocar. The latter had used it on a service to Chobham and it seems probable that Eggleton took the service over from them, running via Kettlewell Hill and Mimbridge to terminate at Burrow Hill at the north end of Chobham. Another Ford bus and two charabancs were owned by mid-1924.

Eggleton was running the charabancs, which probably had folding canvas hoods, on the bus service. In substitution for winter use, he introduced a twelve-seat Renault (AK 1478) in November 1924. This was replaced by April 1925 with a new twenty-seat Republic bus (PE 2505), at which time the Chobham service was extended to West End. In July 1925 another new Republic (PE 7077) arrived, with eighteen-seat bodywork by Woking firm F.W. Coulter. Eggleton's bus garage was at 16 Portugal Road at the rear of his shop, with its end against the side of A & D's Walton Road premises. Eggleton's son, John Edward, born in 1901, joined the business.

It seems that Eggleton also held a licence for the route from Woking to Old Woking and Send but had allowed it to lapse. Whether it had been held since taking over from Woking Autocar is unclear but in September 1925 he reapplied to the council, although as others were established on the route he was not successful. He therefore turned his attention the following month to securing a new service from Woking to Addlestone via Chertsey Road, Six Cross Roads, Woodham and New Haw. This was concurrent to an application by Clifford Ross, who said he would back down if Eggleton were granted the licence as there was insufficient business for two buses. However, in the event neither of them was successful as the council chose to protect Mr Settle's Chertsey service that ran over some of the same ground. Subsequently they did accede to a temporary licence for Eggleton but as he did not start immediately, Settle applied to run to Chertsey via Woodham and Ross asked for his application to be reconsidered. The council's surveyor was charged with meeting all three of them to establish a way forward.

In February 1927 Arthur Locke's fourteen-seat Ford PD 3871 was acquired in readiness for the commencement at last of the Woking to Addlestone service on 7 March, with ten

Acquired by William
Eggleton in July 1925,
this eighteen-seat
Republic (PE 7077) had
a body built in Woking
by F. W. Coulter.
The location is The
Wheatsheaf at West
End. On the right, the
war memorial lists the
names of the village's
fallen in a conflict then
still in recent memory.
(*Peter Trevaskis
Collection*)

A replacement for the
Republic vehicle seen in
the previous photograph
came in March 1931 – a
twenty-seat Dennis GL.
Acquired by London
Transport with the
Addlestone bus service
and three other vehicles
in June 1934, this bus
remained in service with
them until the following
year. (*J. Higham
Collection/Alan Cross*)

PJ 7438, another Dennis
GL, was also acquired
by London Transport
but immediately sold on
to Aldershot & District
with the former Eggleton,
Chobham and West End
service. Numbered D380
by A&D, when disposed
of in 1939 it passed to C.
Walling (Silver Queen)
in Sussex. (*R. Marshall
Collection/East Pennine
Transport Group*)

journeys each way daily. By June that year, when Eggleton applied again unsuccessfully to run from Woking to Old Woking, Send and Ripley, six vehicles were owned. By then, the newsagent's shop in Walton Road had been sold to A. Cooper.

The next new vehicle was PH 5276 in October 1927 – a nineteen-seat Dennis 30 cwt., followed by PH 8572, a twenty-seat Thornycroft A2 in April 1928. The aforementioned Dennis was subject to a complaint from a Mr C. Jermyn Ford of The Old Vicarage, Chobham, who commented that the space between the seats was narrow and the cause of the greatest discomfort to passengers. He suggested that the seat dimensions and spacing were not in accordance with Ministry of Transport specifications and that the bus should not have been licensed, which Eggleton and the council's inspector denied, and the complaint was dismissed. Not all Chobham residents were dissatisfied with Eggleton's buses as it is remembered that drivers would often divert from their route to take those with heavy shopping bags to their doorsteps – very much the epitome of the privately run country bus service. In the early 1930s the usual allocation of vehicles was for two eighteen-seaters to be on the Chobham/West End service and two twenty-seaters on the Addlestone route, with an eighteen-seater as a spare vehicle.

The business was incorporated on 30 April 1928 as W. Eggleton & Son Ltd. In autumn 1928 the Woking to Addlestone service was increased on Saturdays between 1.30 p.m. and 9.30 p.m. to run every thirty minutes. The Eggletons tried to augment their offering in the Addlestone direction by running an additional service via West Byfleet and Byfleet, which would have left the original route at the junction of Woodham Lane and Sheerwater Road and rejoined it at the White Hart in New Haw. The Through Omnibus Services Committee recommended refusal but several further attempts were made, which of course brought forth objections from other operators. However, at the meeting of the Omnibus Sub-Committee on 24 February 1931, it was resolved finally to grant the application, subject to submission of a satisfactory timetable. This was beyond the date when services had to be in existence in order to be considered under the Road Traffic Act for continuation after 1 April 1931, and no request to operate it appeared alongside Eggleton's other licence applications in notices and proceedings in July that year.

Further new vehicles were purchased, all of Dennis manufacture. These were 30 cwt model PG 3194 in September 1929 and GL models PG 8716, PL 5896 and PJ 7438 in April 1930, March 1931 and July 1932 respectively.

In February 1934 London Transport (LT) offered to purchase the Eggleton business for £3,500, as the Woking to Addlestone route fell in their so-called Special Area. However, the Woking to West End service was in A & D's territory, so it would be immediately transferred to them for a sum of £1,357, made up of £556 for Dennis PJ 7438, £771 for the goodwill of the Chobham service, and £30 for a car. The purchase was delayed such that the takeover is recorded as having occurred on 2 June 1934, by which time A & D was to pay £1,277 but without acquiring the car. A & D reorganised their Chobham services from 9 July with the ex-Eggleton journeys being numbered 55C. LT numbered the Addlestone service 456 and acquired Dennis buses PH 5276, PG 3194, PG 8716 and PL 5896, which remained in use until the following year, being sold in April 1936. By 1939 and probably earlier, John Eggleton was a driver for A & D, living at 14 Portugal Road, Woking.

J. R. Fox & Sons
(Woking & District)

The Largest and Most Expansionist Local Operator

Although starting off in a modest way, James Richard Fox's Woking & District firm was to become the largest locally based operator, eventually growing to a size which rivalled A & D's activities in the Woking area. Most of the local operators indulged in unauthorised services and timetables from time to time, but probably the leading exponent was Fox. His version of business development was to flood a route with buses, sometimes with one in front and one behind a competitor, ignoring his timetable as approved by Woking Council and by frequently changing it or supplementing it as he felt fit. There were regular disputes with other firms and Fox was often in trouble with the council, who issued repeated warnings. However, one gains the impression that tolerance was shown, especially when A & D started behaving in a way that appeared to be in the public interest but which challenged the council's regulatory authority. Messrs Fox bombarded the council with continual applications for new and competitive services or variations thereof. By January 1931 they had a fleet of twenty buses and had they not given up the business at that point, one can speculate how they would have adapted, or not, to the more stringent requirements and disciplined orderliness of the Road Traffic Act 1930.

Fox, born at Limehouse in the East End of London in 1879, was a butcher and shopkeeper while living in Mitcham, Surrey. His family consisted of wife Annie, sons James Edward, Stanley, Arthur, Eric and Reginald and daughter Christina. He had also worked for Brooke Bond, delivering tea to shops over a wide area with a horse-drawn van. By 1921 Fox was living at 'Birch' in St Johns Road and must have tested his family's patience when he decided to modify – inside his dining room – a Ford Model T with a touring car body into an eight-seat bus. This took to the road on 1 April 1921 following grant of a licence from Woking Council to use it on the St Johns/Knaphill route. The arrival of a second vehicle a few months later meant that operations could be expanded.

By November 1923 Fox had four small Ford buses, which were kept in outbuildings at the rear of his house. At that point he applied to extend his service from Woking to Kingfield Green, Old Woking and Send, this being granted, while his next move was to extend part of the Knaphill service to Bagshot via Bisley, West End and Lightwater. This was applied for in February 1924 although it may have been running several weeks earlier. Whether this was the catalyst that prompted A & D to extend service 34 to

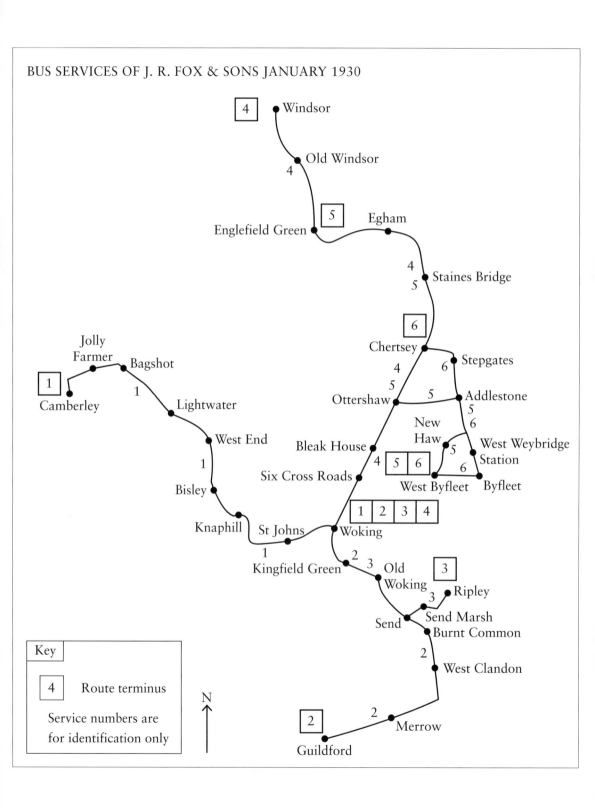

BUS SERVICES OF J. R. FOX & SONS JANUARY 1930

4 — Windsor

4 — Old Windsor

5 — Egham — Englefield Green

4
5 — Staines Bridge

6 — Chertsey — Stepgates
4   6
5   Addlestone
Ottershaw — 5   5
                6
New Haw — West Weybridge Station
5
4 5 6   6
Bleak House — Byfleet
Six Cross Roads — West Byfleet

Jolly Farmer — Bagshot
1 — Camberley
1 — Lightwater
West End
1 — Bisley
Knaphill — St Johns — Woking
1 2 3 4

1 — Kingfield Green
2
3 — Old Woking
3 — Ripley
3
Send — Send Marsh
Burnt Common
2 — West Clandon
2 — Merrow
2 — Guildford

Key

4   Route terminus

Service numbers are
for identification only

N
↑

Bagshot or, if Fox decided to compete subsequent to A & D's proposal, is unclear, but a bus war developed.

By June 1924 Fox was running at least two journeys per hour between Woking and Knaphill as well as un-timetabled extras after 7.30 p.m. Soon afterwards the service to Send was extended to Send Marsh and Ripley, where connections were made with London General's service 115 from Kingston to Guildford. Between February and August 1924, five more Ford Model T fourteen-seat buses, with locally built Perfecta bodies by F. W. Coulter, entered the fleet, some of them replacing earlier vehicles. Their livery was maroon and the fleet name was 'District', although this was subsequently changed to show the full title of 'Woking & District'. As Fox's four eldest sons had joined the business, although not as legal partners, the firm became J. R. Fox & Sons. Stanley had been driving small buses since 1921 when aged sixteen. Two new twenty-seat Berliet vehicles (PD 4089 and PE 1294) arrived in the first quarter of 1925.

On 19 January that year one of the Fords overturned near Bagshot in thick fog. It hit a pile of tarmacadam near the edge of the road, one of its wheels collapsed, and a lady passenger from Lightwater suffered a broken collar bone. In Spring 1925 came two more Fords – saloon bus PE 1870 and fourteen-seat open charabanc PE 2171. Fox apparently intended to use the latter on a competitive service from Woking to Chobham; this was not permitted.

Both Fox and Arthur Smith had been running a shuttle service on Sunday evenings from Brookwood station to Pirbright Camp, using up to ten vehicles. This was to enable military personnel to get back to camp after weekend leave, having arrived on trains from London. This was formally approved by Woking Council in July 1925, accompanied by a request that operations be conducted as quietly as possible as a complaint had been received that the noise disturbed the rest of children and others in Brookwood. In October 1925 the council's surveyor reported that Woking & District had twice altered the timetable on their Woking–Ripley service in the previous three months. They were then running an unsanctioned extra nine journeys as far as Send, making a total of twenty-six in all. The timetable had been arranged to run a few minutes in front of London General service 79 between Woking and Old Woking. In addition, Fox

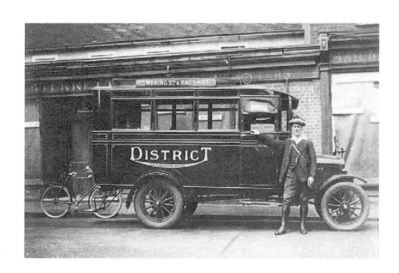

Typical of the Ford Model Ts operated by Woking & District in the early 1920s, this example shows the steps that facilitated passenger access by a door at the rear. Adjacent to it stands Jim Fox's son, Stanley, who was heavily involved in the business with his brothers. (*Iain Wakeford Collection*)

Another view of a Fox Ford T with the 'District' fleet name, before the trading title was changed to Woking & District. Fox had several of his Fords bodied locally by F. W. Coulter under the 'Perfecta' brand name and this may have been one of them. (*G. Robbins Collection/Alan Cross*)

had saturated the Woking–Knaphill route by running fifty-four journeys outwards (as opposed to the fourteen originally applied for) and forty-one journeys inwards, against the authorised fifteen. On 15 August 1925 the surveyor made observations in Hermitage Road between 2 p.m. and 10 p.m. Twenty-six buses from various firms passed him by empty and thirty-nine had five or less passengers. Frequently there were five buses in his view at one time!

Fox's irregularities were noted by the council's inspector. On 16 August 1925 the Ford charabanc (which was not licensed by the council) was collecting soldiers at Brookwood station for Pirbright Camp, with 'private' on the indicator board, while buses were running from Woking to West End at unauthorised times. On 31 August a Fox vehicle turned short of its terminus (at The Garibaldi in Knaphill) at The Anchor and then picked up passengers for Woking who ordinarily would have travelled on another firm's bus. In September, some of Fox's drivers did not go to the rear of the Woking station rank on arrival, but to the front, touted passengers for St Johns out of another waiting bus and then departed at an unscheduled time.

On an unspecified occasion one source recalled that allegedly Fox blocked St Johns Road, outside his garage, with buses to prevent other buses running to schedule. There was a later occasion, in 1930, when relative William Henry Fox was fined for causing an obstruction on the highway by parking several buses on St Johns Road near the garage for two hours every morning. He claimed that as there was so little room in the garage premises, it was necessary to do this as part of preparing the buses for service.

In September 1925 Fox applied to renew licences for eight buses, and although the council would only grant licences for five, there was no reduction in operations. The application stated eighteen journeys to Bagshot, four more as far as West End, an extra twenty-seven as far as Knaphill and seventeen to Send or Ripley. Fox arranged to see the council's surveyor and inspector on 2 November, with a view to setting timetables that were in the public interest, although it is unlikely that anything changed unless it was in the firm's interest.

Although a final fourteen-seat Ford T (PE 8157) was delivered in January 1926, Fox switched his vehicle ordering to Daimler, purchasing twenty-six-seat CM36 models in November 1925 and February 1926 (PE 6984 and 8642) and twenty-seat CK36 model PE 9993 in March 1926. These replaced some of the earlier Fords. The twenty-seat Daimler was apparently ordered specially for use on the Ripley service and had a shortened chassis to ease negotiation of a sharp and narrow corner in Old Woking. When A & D increased the frequency of their service 34 on 25 February 1926, Fox immediately abandoned the timetable on his Bagshot service to run just a few minutes in front of A & D. He also applied for four extra licences to run from Woking to Sunningdale and Windlesham, which was refused as the existing services were felt to be adequate. His next move came on 9 March when he asked for two new licences for Windlesham/Sunningdale, two for Deepcut and Frimley (to compete with Arthur Smith) and six as 'reserves'. These were also refused as not being necessary to satisfy the public need.

Other firms continually complained about Woking & District running just in front of them and heated disputes between drivers. Meanwhile, the council's surveyor had been attempting to broker an agreement between Fox and A & D that unfortunately resulted in deadlock and Fox introducing yet more journeys on the Knaphill service where some journeys were as little as five minutes apart. Relations with the council were further strained when the clerk took out two summons against Fox for employing an unlicensed driver, with the firm being fined £1 for each. The hackney carriage inspector had observed George Garland, who, having driven lorries previously, did not hold a licence. Fox pleaded ignorance of this and stated that Garland had only been driving when accompanied by son Stanley Fox to supervise him.

The inspector then reported on the conduct of Jim Fox Jr at Knaphill on 17 April, which had been followed by a letter complaining about the inspector. The council took a dim view of this – unless the letter was withdrawn and Fox apologised for his conduct to the inspector, they would not renew any licences. It appears he did not do so in a way felt satisfactory, and for this alleged lack of respect to a council official, it was suggested that his driver's licence should be revoked. He eventually withdrew the letter and apologised to the inspector for what had happened whereupon his licence was renewed.

The council continued its attempts in summer 1926 to broker an agreement between the various firms running to Knaphill and on towards Bagshot. They should agree on regular-interval timetables in the public interest and avoid running buses so close

By 1925, vehicle design had moved forward considerably. Number 8 in the Woking & District fleet was PE 6984, a twenty-six-seat Daimler CM36 new in November that year. It appears to be on the Woking–Guildford service. It ended up in London Transport's service until sold in 1934 to a lady at Shoreham-by-Sea for use as a caravan. (*G. Robbins Collection/Alan Cross*)

together that they were useless to passengers and caused unnecessary traffic congestion. The firms eventually agreed to meet at the A & D offices in Aldershot to coordinate timetables giving a bus about every ten minutes, on the basis of A & D running forty-three journeys on various services and Fox running thirty-two, while Renshaw & Leam were to run sixteen and Hampton sixteen. The agreed starting date was 1 August. Fox was then censured for not seeking approval for extra journeys on his Ripley service that had been increased to half-hourly in July 1926. Subsequently, officials from London General were seen surveying the Ripley route, which concerned Fox as he felt his service was adequate and some journeys ran at a loss.

In January 1927 Fox turned his competitive attentions to the east of Woking when he applied for an hourly service to Chertsey via Woodham, New Haw and Addlestone. As others ran over parts of this route, the application was refused, as was one for a service to Guildford via Westfield and Mayford. Further unsuccessful attempts were made in 1927 to run to Chertsey. However, this did not prevent the introduction soon afterwards of a service between West Byfleet, New Haw, Addlestone and Chertsey although subsequent attempts to make it reach Woking via Woodham and to link it to a Send service on an hourly basis were unsuccessful due to objections.

In March 1927 Fox was fined £5 for using a bus with another bus's excise licence disc displayed on it. One of the Berliet vehicles was off the road on 18 December 1926 with a broken axle, so a mechanic gave instructions for a Ford T to be substituted at short notice. As the Ford had no tax disc, one was transferred from the Berliet.

Since at least June 1927 two of the afternoon Woking to Knaphill journeys were diverted through the grounds of Brookwood Mental Hospital for hospital visitors, not only missing out part of the normal route but also returning from Knaphill to Woking five minutes after the scheduled times, thus encroaching on the times of the next buses. Fox was told to cease the practice immediately but in September permission was granted for a bespoke service solely serving the hospital. However, refusal was given to his application to run to Send every fifteen minutes on Fridays and Saturdays, although from October 1927 the Sunday service on the Ripley route was doubled to half-hourly. Vehicle intake in 1927 for Woking & District consisted of two Thornycroft A1s in February and the largest bus to date – a Tilling Stevens B10A2 with thirty-two-seat bodywork by Wilton – in December.

The conductor got the blame when the last Woking & District journey to Ripley on New Year's Eve 1927 went no further than Send and the passengers had to get off and walk through a snowstorm to get home. Perhaps the crew wanted to get home too in time to see the New Year in.

On 1 March 1928 Fox submitted applications to the council for a new hourly Woking to Guildford service via Mayford, to be worked as an extension of the Bagshot–Woking service and again for a Chertsey–Woodham–Woking-Send service. Fox claimed he had 123 signatures from the residents of Walton Road, Woking in support of the latter and there had been repeated requests from users of the Chertsey–West Byfleet service for it to be extended to Woking. These new ventures would duplicate various other services of Eggleton, Martin, A & D, London General and Locke, who all objected, thus the applications were refused. With the tension between A & D and Fox heightening, both parties repeatedly complained about each other.

For about three months in 1928, Woking & District, like A & D, experimented with an express service, possibly unlicensed, from Woking to London with one round trip each day. Being no match for the choice offered by the local rail service, it was unprofitable. Fox wanted to develop it into a more attractive hourly service but the council vetoed this. Another attempt to gain a local licence for a service to London was refused in July 1930 as Woking Council was still trying to limit the number of buses on the streets of the town.

Fox was running two journeys per hour out to Send. One of these continued to Ripley and permission was granted by the Guildford Watch Committee in September 1928 to extend the one that terminated at Send to Burnt Common, West Clandon, Merrow and Guildford. This was joined the following month by a competitive service run by East Surrey from Send to Guildford numbered 31. However, Fox's application to run a further two journeys each hour as far as Send was refused in November as being unnecessary, as no doubt Woking Council envisaged further lines of buses as seen on the St Johns route. To round off 1928, Fox unsuccessfully applied to run from Woking to Chertsey via Ottershaw, after the matter had been considered by the first meeting of the new Conference on Through Omnibus Services on 30 October. 1928 had seen two new buses into the Woking & District fleet – a Thornycroft LB in March and another thirty-two-seat Tilling Stevens B10A2 in November.

William Moore, aged nineteen, who started working for Fox in February 1929, took the firm to court in August that year for alleged wrongful dismissal without notice. He was employed as a trainee mechanic from 6.30 a.m. to 5 p.m. seven days a week, for a wage of 30s a week. He stated he had worked much unpaid overtime and if he finished his normal duties he would be found a task in the yard or in the house. The final straw was on 27 June when he was expected to work into the evening to help replace the back axle of a vehicle that was due to be used on a trip to the coast next day. Jim Fox said that Moore had been dismissed for disobedience. There were no set hours of work and if men stayed after 5 p.m., tea was provided for them. Moore had apparently never complained before, had a day off to go to The Derby horse race and was just asked to stay behind to help with repairing the coach. The Bench, feeling sympathetic, commented that the conditions of employment sounded like a military order and awarded Moore £1 8s 6d damages and 3s 6d costs.

1929 was the year that relations between A & D and Woking & District seemed to reach their nadir, with Fox indulging in some aggressive empire-building and acquiring another seven new buses: five Thornycroft A2Ls and two Thornycroft BCs. The last Fords were removed from the fleet. Originally proposed by Fox in January 1929 was a grandiose through service between Guildford and Egham via West Clandon, Send, Woking, Ottershaw, Chertsey and the west side of Staines Bridge. By May this idea had extended beyond Egham to Englefield Green, Old Windsor and Windsor. Between Woking and Chertsey the route was changed to run via Woodham, Byfleet and Addlestone. Unwilling to let the matter drop, he also renewed his desire for extra journeys on existing services. The Windsor application was referred to the Through Omnibus Services Joint Advisory Committee, which recommended Woking Council to refuse it. Although the latter did decide to grant a Woking–Windsor service to Fox in July, probably as a warning to A & D who were out of favour with the council,

A very smart addition to Fox's fleet in March 1928 was No 14, a Thornycroft LB. It carried a Hampshire registration mark (OT 7822) so was probably registered by Thornycrofts in Basingstoke. (*Alan Lambert Collection*)

In the winter of 1928/9, the body building firm of Wilton of Croydon supplied two vehicles to Fox; one (seen here) was VB 4060, a Tilling Stevens B10A2. The other was VB 4550, a Thornycroft A2L. The location is North Street, Guildford. (*W. Noel Jackson/Alan Cross*)

Fox had already introduced a direct service from Woking to Ottershaw and Chertsey on 1 June 1929. At the same time the West Byfleet to Chertsey service was diverted via Ottershaw and extended to Staines Bridge and Egham. On 20 July the Chertsey service was extended hourly to Egham and Windsor. On that day, Stan Fox recalled that 100 passengers were waiting to travel, so relief buses had to be summoned from St Johns.

An enraged A & D fought back on 16 August 1929 with their own unlicensed Woking–Chertsey direct service 48B, to which Fox responded by extending his Bagshot service to Camberley three days later, competing with a further section of A & D service 34. For good measure the Woking & District West Byfleet–Egham service was extended to Englefield Green from the same date, but halved in frequency beyond Chertsey. Both of Fox's services to Chertsey just happened to run a few minutes ahead of A & D over shared sections of route! Woking Council was quite unable to keep up with this breathless chain of events, partially ultra vires of their authority.

Most of the Woking & District service development in 1930 occurred outside of the Woking area. Around December 1929 an additional service competing with Martin's Bus de Ville and W. Eggleton was started from West Byfleet to Chertsey via Byfleet, West Weybridge station, New Haw (White Hart), Addlestone and Stepgates but had ceased by August 1930 as licences were not granted due to objections. From 1 April that year the West Byfleet to Englefield Green service was extended to Old Windsor and Windsor, forming a joint half-hourly operation with the Woking–Windsor service over the common section of route north of Ottershaw. An extension beyond Windsor to Maidenhead had earlier been refused, as was a proposal to divert some journeys on West Byfleet–Englefield Green at Egham to Sunningdale, perhaps due to the presence of A & D service 1 along the A30 road. Fox reconstituted his business as a limited company, with J. R. Fox & Sons Ltd being registered on 26 May 1930.

Fox's final application came in September 1930 to run from Woking to Brookwood station via Horsell and Knaphill, over A & D territory. The latter was negotiating to buy the W & D business so perhaps Fox intended this to encourage A & D to reach a favourable agreement. In any event it was inevitably refused a licence in November as of course it clashed with existing services.

No less than five new buses arrived with W & D in May 1930. These were four more thirty-two-seat Tilling Stevens B10A2s, this time with bodywork by Petty, and a twenty-six-seat AJS Pilot, also bodied by Petty.

As early as April 1928, Fox had offered his business to A & D but his asking price of £25,000 was declined in June. Negotiations continued but were abandoned in March 1929, following which Fox intensified his competitive campaign. Eventually agreement was reached in October 1930 for Fox's original asking price, so his tenacity was rewarded. Thus, Woking & District ceased trading on 12 January 1931, being acquired by A & D but with a major part of it being immediately sold on to London General. Further details of the acquisition process and afterwards are given in the chapters relating to those companies. As a final gesture, Fox apparently assembled all his buses and many of his eighty-strong staff to be photographed at The Triangle (between St Johns and Woking) on the Sunday morning prior to the take-over.

The Woking & District business must have been doing well as Jim Fox purchased eight new vehicles in 1929 to supplement his fleet and to replace earlier buses. Six of them were Thornycrofts with bodies supplied by Nottingham firm Challands Ross. The first of these was PG 1099, an A2L model, seen here after being transferred by subsequent owner London General to run in the Sevenoaks area. (*Alan Lambert Collection*)

Next to arrive were a pair of robust-looking Thornycroft BC thirty-two-seaters. PG 1757 is seen prior to delivery to Woking and had Challands Ross 'Enchantress' bodywork. (*Alan Lambert Collection*)

The other Thornycroft BC new in July 1929 was PG 1758. When part of the Fox business was acquired by London General, this vehicle was among those that continued to be used for a time in the Woking area, but has been captured later, working on a Slough local service, from Windsor garage. (*J. Higham Collection/Alan Cross*)

The second Thornycroft A2L of 1929 (PG 2018), with Challands Ross 'Emerald' body style, was one of four similar Fox vehicles which were operated by Newbury & District Motor Services from January 1937, after sale by London Transport. (*Alan Lambert Collection*)

PG 4226 was the fourth of the 1929 twenty-seat Thornycrofts and, prior to delivery to Woking & District, was exhibited by Thornycroft at the Commercial Motor Show at Olympia in London. (*Alan Lambert Collection*)

Matching anything operated by Aldershot & District, Fox purchased four Tilling Stevens B10A2s with Petty bodywork in May 1930. PG 9384 is seen here with a coastal resort on the destination display. When Woking & District was sold to A&D, the latter only retained five buses, all Tilling Stevens B10A2s, as they already had the type in their fleet. PG 9382 subsequently passed to Blue Motor Services of Boarhunt, Hants. (*Eric Nixon Collection*)

The final vehicle into the Woking & District fleet was PG 9385, a twenty-six-seat AJS Pilot with rear-entrance bodywork by Petty. Passing to London General, here it works service 29 (Newdigate–Dorking) on the Saturday extension to South Holmwood, sometime in the early 1930s. (*J. Higham Collection/Alan Cross*)

Fox Senior moved to Horsell. Recalling his past career and emulating bus proprietors Frank Renshaw, John Hampton and Stanley Tanner, by 1935 he had opened a butcher's shop at 128 High Street in Old Woking with delivery vans painted in the same maroon colour scheme as used for the Woking & District buses. In 1931, Stan Fox joined A & D as an inspector while Jim, Eric and Arthur Fox went to work for London General. Stan subsequently operated taxis and set up a driving school and ran that business for many years as S. R. Fox & Sons – Woking School of Motoring, while other family members also became driving instructors.

A. H. Stilwell and H. E. S. Trigg

Two Owner-Drivers Bring the Bus to Sutton Green

In the early 1920s there were still some opportunities to establish bus services along secondary routes into the nearest local towns, in advance of territorial consolidation by the larger bus companies. Many local men thought they would try their luck by earning a living as an owner-driver by providing a bus service for their local community. At that time, employment prospects for the huge number of men who had been discharged from the armed forces into a civilian life 'fit for heroes' were not necessarily bright.

One such person was Arthur Henry Stilwell of 4 Crabtree Cottages, Jacobs Well, near Guildford. In July 1921 he successfully applied for a licence from Woking and Guildford Councils for a twelve-seat Napier bus, registered PB 8935. This was used to start a service from Guildford to Woking via Stoke, Jacobs Well, Sutton Green, Westfield and Kingfield Green, on Mondays to Saturdays with five round trips. However, he found two of the trips unremunerative, so he reduced his service to three round trips on Mondays to Fridays and four on Saturdays.

In May 1922, the Napier vehicle was sold to John Hampton and Stilwell replaced it with PB 6848, a Republic of unknown capacity and probably acquired second-hand. It seems that Stilwell settled down with his service, causing little concern to anybody. In June 1924 it was noted by Woking Council that he ran the service punctually and satisfactorily. By then, the service on Wednesdays had been reduced to one round trip in the morning which was Guildford-orientated, allowing one hour and ten minutes in that town.

Stilwell was somewhat dismayed when he learnt of an application by Edward Trigg to operate a daily hourly service for most of the day over the same route between Guildford and Woking. Another owner-driver, Trigg intended to use one bus with a three-minute turnaround time at each end of the route. It was on 16 September 1924 that Henry Edward Stapleton Trigg of 47 Farnham Road, Guildford wrote to Guildford Council's town clerk to apply for a licence. He advised him that Rice & Harper had an order in hand for a new fourteen-seat bus, probably a Ford, which was registered PD 3376. Trigg considered his service to be far more comprehensive and beneficial than Stilwell's and pledged to adhere to his timetable. He said he had no wish to harm his opponent's trade or to run just in front of him and was willing to make any adjustments that the Watch Committee thought appropriate. Trigg's bus was licensed by Guildford Council from 4 November 1924 but an application in October for a licence in Woking was refused on

Between 1921 and 1924, this Napier twelve-seat bus (PB 8935) was used by Arthur Stilwell and then John Hampton. There is a suggestion that for a short time in 1924 it was also run by John Denyer. Whether the driver in this view is one of those proprietors, and if so which one, is uncertain. (*G. Robbins Collection/ Alan Cross*)

the grounds that the council thought that Stilwell's service was adequate, despite the eighty-six-signature petition from Jacobs Well and Sutton Green that Trigg sent to them. Despite this setback, Trigg seems to have started his service, at least between Guildford and Sutton Green, ignoring a warning from Woking Council that he must not ply for hire in their area. However, they relented in December and granted a licence for the whole route. Trigg traded as the Royal Blue Bus Service.

By then, Stilwell was living with his parents at the Robin Hood public house near Knaphill and in his letters to the Chief Constable of Guildford he pointed out that he depended entirely on his bus for his income. Without the appearance of Trigg, it was already difficult to get a living from the service as parts of the route were also served by P. Crouch, A & D and London General. This left him as the unique operator through Jacobs Well and Sutton Green, with a small population of mainly farm workers who could only afford to go shopping by bus about twice a week.

In February 1925, Trigg acquired a second bus and revised his timetable. The next development was an application in December 1925 from Arthur Locke of Guildford for a forty-five-minute-interval service using two buses over the same route as Stilwell and Trigg. Guildford Council did not reach a decision immediately and in the meantime, P. Crouch & Son applied to run out from Guildford as far as Sutton Green, neither of which moved Woking Council. In February 1926, complaints were received regarding irregularities in Trigg's service. By then he only had one bus and if it broke down the service became, in his word, disorganised, which means it did not run. Trigg decided to capitulate and withdrew his service from 1 March 1926 and probably after a short period, Locke started his new service, although Woking Council did not agree to licence it until the end of May by which time it may have physically started.

Locke soon had the route to himself as Arthur Stilwell stopped operating from 2 July 1926. By February 1926 both Stilwell and Trigg had approached A & D to buy them out, but this does not seem to have occurred. However, Stilwell was offered a job as a driver by A & D. The next that is heard of him is in August 1930, by which time he was living at Stockers Lane in Kingfield Green. As an A & D driver, he accidentally knocked down and killed a man in St Johns. However, the inquest recorded a verdict of misadventure on the part of the victim, with no evidence of negligent driving by Stilwell.

Interlude –
The Men From the Council

Much material on bus service matters has been gleaned from the Minutes of Woking Urban District Council Highways Committee and its Omnibus Sub-Committee. In this chapter we look at a few of the more generic matters relating to local bus services. The Minutes cast some light on the amount of work and correspondence that council officials were obliged to undertake in the quest of elected members to exercise their powers to attempt to control errant bus proprietors. The latter were much more concerned with maximising their revenue and gaining commercial advantage than taking part in coordination activities.

Under the Town Police Clauses Act, urban and borough councils were given powers to licence hackney carriages. After the horse-drawn era, this crossed over to motor taxis and omnibuses, with local licences being issued to vehicles (attached to a specific service in some cases), drivers and conductors. However, these powers did not extend to rural district councils and even in the town areas, different councils chose to exercise different levels of control over bus services. For the operator, the frustration was that longer-distance services might require licences from more than one urban area, with the various authorities sometimes taking different decisions as to whether to issue licences or not. This made cohesive service development difficult, while a village-based operator might be able to pick up passengers locally without restriction but might not have been able to gain a licence from the council in the town that his passengers wanted to access. All of the foregoing came to an end as far as buses were concerned in 1931 with the implementation of the Road Traffic Act 1930. Henceforth, services would be approved by a traffic commissioner taking a wider view, instead of local councillors taking a parochial or protective approach.

Apart from the councillors themselves, those involved in administering bus services in Woking were principally the clerk, the surveyor and the hackney carriage inspector, while in Guildford the Watch Committee was advised by the Chief Constable. To try and keep operators in check, Woking Council only issued vehicle licences for short periods – a few weeks or a few months, although the threat of having licences revoked for a misdemeanour was usually more latent than actual! The post of hackney carriage inspector was by no means a sinecure.

There follows a selection of paraphrased snippets from the Minutes and other sources that are generally self-explanatory and show what the council and its officials had to face in the routine conduct of business. Author's comments are in brackets.

27 *April 1917*: The Chairman of the Highways Committee had visited St Johns to ascertain the best position for a Stand for omnibuses. The committee recommends that

the space between the horse-trough and the path be used for two omnibuses to stand.

1 July 1921: Forty-six motor cars and motor buses had been inspected for the purpose of renewal of licences. Of those, twenty-five required certain repairs to be carried out.

3 February 1922: Messrs Renshaw, Bullman and Smith were reminded that a lamp of sufficient strength and placing was necessary to provide interior illumination for the reasonable convenience of passengers.

30 May 1924: In every bus should be posted a timetable. Buses belonging to one proprietor and running on a particular route should start from the Station in the order that they are standing on the Rank and timetables should not be arranged so a bus runs immediately before another is due to depart.

27 June 1924: The roads in the district are narrow and although it is necessary to licence ample buses for public requirements, those surplus to demand should not be licensed as they only add to congestion of streets, without serving any useful purpose.

April 1925: The council was considering the appointment of a hackney carriage inspector (to try and keep order on the road) at a salary of £80 per year. One councillor suggested that a 'man of tact and fairness was needed – perhaps a retired policeman'. There was some light-hearted dissent: 'Why not a retired schoolmaster?'

29 May 1925: The committee at their last meeting granted a licence to Mr Cripps for fourteen-seat Fiat open charabanc CR 6831, subject to Mr Cripps stating the intended use of the vehicle. He replied that his idea was to ply for hire in Pirbright and Bisley Camps during the shooting season but not on a regular route. Mr Cripps to be informed he must define his route and submit a regular timetable. (The committee seems to have missed the point that this would be an ad hoc operation. He survived whatever 'shooting' took place as in November he unsuccessfully applied to run from Brookwood station to Pirbright Camp at weekends.)

31 July 1925: The inspector reported that the number of daily bus journeys between Woking and Knaphill on weekdays was 104. Certain proprietors had licences for more buses than were required by them to run their authorised timetables. The number of licences should be reduced; the current surplus encouraged pirating and was liable to cause traffic congestion. The inspector suggested that buses should not exceed 12 mph when passing a school and should never exceed 15 mph. Cllr Mrs Lakeman said that if buses kept to their scheduled timetables, there would be no need for excessive speed. She had recently seen three buses 'on each other's back wheels'.

2 October 1925: There is undoubtedly considerable ill feeling between the proprietors. The timetables in many cases are frequently altered with a view to getting in front of each other, with chaotic results. Cllr Gower had seen twenty-three buses lined up in Maybury Road and Duke Street and a driver due to depart had been boxed in on either side and could not move to depart. Cllr Renshaw defended the proprietors – a bus cost about £400 and they had a living to earn. Cllr Marrett said that one man applied for eight licences and got five, another asked for five and got two, some asked for two and got two. He queried the logic of this and opined that the largest proportion was granted to the man who gave the inspector the most trouble. (That would probably have been J. R. Fox).

9 April 1926: The inspector reported that since A & D had started running hourly from Guildford to Yorktown at reduced fares, competition between Woking and Knaphill had been very keen, while the undertaking to maintain a regular service has been

A closer view of three of Frank Mills' small vehicles with canvas gas bags during the First World War. PA 7163 was recorded by Woking Council at least twice as being of Singer manufacture but it does look suspiciously similar to the two other vehicles, which were recorded as Fords. CD 2597 on the right was little more than a large car but no doubt appeared on the St Johns service. (*G. Robbins Collection/Alan Cross*)

One of Guildford & District's 1914 Dennis vehicles on the short-lived Guildford–Woking–Walton on Thames service, probably photographed in that year. A potential location is New Haw. (*David Barker/Peter Holmes Collections*)

One of Aldershot & District's Strachan-bodied Tilling Stevens, B10A2s (OU 7954), seems to have been abandoned across a road junction on service 48A to Camberley. Judging by the puddle of water on the road, it may have a radiator leak following a minor collision. (*Mike Stephens Collection*)

disregarded. The service has also been disrupted as one firm gave no service for five whole days and seven part days during March 1926. These circumstances made it most difficult for him to impose control.

During April 1926 the volume of detailed consideration that the Highways Committee had to give to bus service matters had become so great that a separate Omnibus Sub-Committee was set up.

2 July 1926: The running of buses during June has been unsatisfactory, the majority of proprietors taking their vehicles off the routes at times for work of a private character. The timetable for Woking–Knaphill was almost entirely disregarded and but for the hourly A & D bus, the service would be chaotic.

September 1926: The Woking to Knaphill service was reported as running satisfactorily (no doubt this was to everybody's amazement). Cllr Matthews said 'this was one of the best bits of news they had heard for a long time'.

1 October 1926: The inspector drew attention to the increasing practice of passengers (mostly women) being permitted to sit on the right hand side of the driver. The driver would be unable to give the appropriate hand signals to his offside without inconveniencing the passenger to his right.(Certain small buses, including some imported Ford T chassis, were left-hand-drive.)

December 1926: The surveyor reported that he was proceeding with the erection of signs indicating stopping places for the various bus routes.

29 April 1927: The clerk had written to the proprietors, informing them that they must obey the instructions of the inspector and treat him with proper respect. The committee is determined to only grant licences to those who run their buses in a way that is satisfactory to them.

14 February 1928: Having considered A & D's proposals for more buses from Woking to Knaphill and Guildford via Horsell and Lower Knaphill, some councillors thought that preference was being given by the Sub-Committee to A & D over local proprietors. Cllr Quartermaine denied this and said it was very hard to strike a balance between the commercial aspirations of the operators and the public need. Cllr Renshaw thought it right that other proprietors should be asked to give their observations before any service was granted but added that 'the proprietors had never agreed among themselves and never would'.

29 May 1928: Proprietors of omnibuses who propose to run a journey through this (Woking) council's district but starting and finishing at towns outside the district, sometimes apply for licences from them before applying to this council. In other cases it may affect this district only slightly and may be of importance to the towns from which the route starts or finishes. The committee recommend that the Royal Borough of Windsor, the Urban District Councils of Egham, Windlesham, Bracknell and Chertsey and the Borough of Guildford be written to and asked whether they will inform this council of a route that will affect the Woking area, before granting licences themselves in respect of their areas. They should also state whether it is of importance to them that the route is worked and give this council an opportunity to express its views.

31 July 1928: (In granting licences to A & D vehicles without local inspection, the council sought confirmation that they complied with Ministry of Transport requirements, that they were insured against third party risks, fitted with pneumatic tyres and would only be run on routes in the district and to timetables that were approved by the council. However, A & D were unwilling to sign up to the latter requirement).

> We consider that it is the function of the bus operator to fix the times at which vehicles should run. In the case of a company such as this, who are running services over wide areas, the timetables have to be planned with the greatest of care and thought, so as to connect with other services and in many cases to provide through services between various districts. We feel sure that your council will appreciate that if the various councils in our operating area endeavoured to control timings, it would be impossible to work these services. The other twenty or so councils have recognised this fact and have not attached conditions to licences. The company fully appreciates the desire of the council to coordinate services and we feel sure your council also appreciates what the company has done to achieve this coordination, both in spirit and letter.

The clerk had responded, saying, 'If your company were allowed to run their buses at their pleasure over any route or at any time it would lead to confusion, as every other proprietor would naturally wish to have the same free hand. The council has always dealt with matters in a reasonable manner. It is only by the council exercising some control that chaos can be avoided'.

(Woking Council failed to be moved by the wider issues raised by A & D and continued to insist that every route and timing must be approved by them or licences would not be issued or renewed. Similarly, London General was becoming frustrated by the council's controlling aspirations of their service, which had already been approved by the London Area Licensing Authority under the London Traffic Act 1924. This was not readily accepted by the council, either.)

30 October 1928: Having consulted the adjoining authorities over licensing matters, it was eventually decided that a Joint Conference on Through Omnibus Services be held. The first meeting was on this date, prior to the Omnibus Sub-Committee and was hosted by Woking Council and attended by representatives from Windlesham and Egham Urban Districts and from Chertsey Rural District Council. Their first recommendations, which were adopted subsequently by Woking Council although it was under no obligation to do so, were: the application from A & D to extend their Woking to Maybury Inn service to Weybridge be refused; the application from A & D to extend the Maybury Inn service to Send and Guildford be granted; the application from Messrs Fox to run from Woking to Chertsey be refused, and the application from London General to run a service from Kingston to Guildford via Addlestone, Woking and Send also be refused.

27 November 1928: Two meetings of the Joint Conference had been held and it had been decided to set up a Regional Advisory Committee, with two representatives from each of the interested authorities being invited. (This manifested itself into the Woking & District Through Omnibus Services Joint Advisory Committee. Such a body was highly unusual at that time and was possibly unique, at least in southern England.)

October 1929: (The council had issued a new Undertaking which it required all operators to sign. Among other things it obliged operators to adhere to timetables and routes agreed with the council. Even A & D signed it). Councillor Quartermaine said he 'did not want it to be thought that the committee was hostile to buses. A well-regulated

Woking & District's brand new Thornycroft LB, OT 7822, was no doubt considered state-of-the-art in 1928. Passing to London General on the sale of the Fox business, it lasted until sale by London Transport in January 1936. (*Alan Lambert Collection*)

Photographed before delivery, PG 2018, one of Woking & District's four Thornycroft A2L/Challand Ross buses, may well have turned a few heads in Woking in 1929 as a great improvement on the last of Jim Fox's primitive Ford Ts and Berliets. (*Alan Lambert Collection*)

Standing outside Arthur Locke's Blue Saloon Coaches garage in Guildford is either CPA 875 or CPE 222, a neat Guy Wolf with Beadle twenty-seat bodywork. (*Malcolm Lambley Collection*)

service was of benefit to the trading community and a convenience to the public. It was the council's business to encourage and work in harmony with proprietors. They had aimed all along at supervision, not interference.' (Doubtless the operators would have argued differently.)

29 October 1929: The Joint Committee thought it essential that the operator's name be printed on bus tickets (rather than just using 'stock' issues), following a complaint that a proprietor had refused to accept a return ticket actually issued by him!

27 January 1931: Councillor Quartermaine was unsuccessful with his nomination to become a traffic commissioner in the South Eastern Traffic Area. The hackney carriage inspector, Mr J. Coomber had applied to work for the Ministry of Transport. Considering the impending changes in licensing arrangements, the council strongly recommended him to pursue the job application in view of his extensive experience of licensing matters gained while working in Woking.

31 March 1931: (The clerk formally reported the amendments to legislation that took licensing matters for omnibuses, routes, drivers and conductors away from local authorities into the jurisdiction of the traffic commissioners. The last recorded bus service application considered by the Omnibus Sub-Committee before it was disbanded seems to have been from W. Eggleton Ltd for adjustments and additional journeys on the Woking–West End service, which were granted.)

8 December 1931: The pioneering and useful coordination activities of the Through Omnibus Services Joint Advisory Committee had been suspended since the traffic commissioners took over on 1 April. It was therefore proposed to disband it. Cllr Quartermaine commented that it remained to be seen whether the new arrangements proved more efficient than the Joint Committee. There was regret from some that bus licensing matters were now out of local hands and that the proceedings of the commissioners were often held at locations somewhat distant from Woking. The new licence fees and operators' legal costs for representation in the traffic court would have to come from the fares revenue, meaning there was little chance of fares being reduced. Those who were involved with the Joint Committee were thanked for their efforts and Woking Council was thanked for its hospitality in hosting the meetings. If it had achieved nothing else, the committee had fostered a good relationship between the adjoining authorities. (It was the end of an era and the end of time-consuming work for officers and elected members alike.)

P. R. Burton,
H. Settle & B. H. Martin

... And Several Might-Have-Beens on the Byfleet Road

During 1921 the mighty London General Omnibus Co. had been advising the council of its intentions to extend its service from Kingston to West Byfleet through to Woking. Although licences for ten single-deck vehicles were granted in July, various delays meant that service 79 did not reach Woking until 4 January 1922. In the meantime a local operator decided to open up services in the direction of General's proposed territory.

A Mr P. R. Burton, whose address was given as Highcroft on Maybury Hill, just outside Woking, applied successfully in September 1921 for a licence for a new twenty-seat vehicle of unknown make, registered PC 5209. Burton also used the address of Woking Automobile Engineering Works, Maybury Road, which is where the vehicle may have been kept. The route applied for was from Woking to Walton on Thames via Maybury Inn, West Byfleet, Byfleet Village, New Haw, Addlestone and Weybridge. The licence was formally granted in mid-October.

However, a surviving undated timetable folder suggests that the bus instead ran on two routes from Woking to Addlestone, either via Ottershaw or via Woodham and New Haw, before continuing to either Weybridge or Chertsey. Certain journeys operated direct from Chertsey to Weybridge via Addlestone. There were four through journeys from Woking to Weybridge or Chertsey on Mondays to Fridays with a considerably enhanced service on Saturday afternoons, when most journeys terminated at Addlestone and Weybridge was not served. The timetable folder advertises that the vehicle was available for hire in the evenings for dance parties etc. at a moderate charge and a handwritten addition gives the name Blue Motor Coach.

Despite the services of London General and Mr Burton, a Mr A. Coldicutt of Mill Lane, Byfleet applied in December 1922 for a licence to run a covered Mercedes motor lorry as a passenger-carrying vehicle between Woking and Addlestone, but no further reference to this has been found.

Burton's operations were replaced in September 1923 by H. Settle of 75 Guildford Street, Chertsey. His service is believed to have run to Addlestone by the same route as quoted in Burton's original application and then on to Chertsey via Stepgates. Settle also acquired Burton's vehicle for which a licence was granted to him on 9 October 1923. Just over a month later, Woking Council received an application from another proprietor who had designs on Settle's route – James Henry Absolem Weaver of Slough.

SMALL OPERATORS' SERVICES TOWARDS
ADDLESTONE AND CHERTSEY

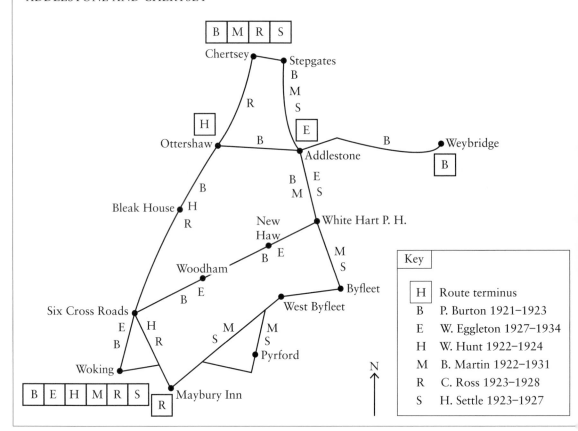

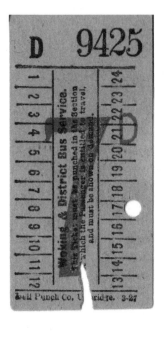

In 1921 James Weaver was already running buses under the title of Slough & District, including on the route between Slough and Windsor. He was based at Hampden Motor Works in Ledgers Road, Slough. Apparently keen to expand his activities, he started a satellite operation in Surrey by commencing a service on 4 November 1922 from Guildford to Wonersh in competition with A & D and some small local operators. This was run under the District Omnibus Service title. In November 1923 he applied to Woking Council for licences for four buses: fourteen-seaters, registered BH 5023/8471/8891, of which at least the latter two were Ford Ts, and AEC B-type twenty-seater PP 491. These were to be used on services from Woking to Byfleet, New Haw and Addlestone and to Ripley via Old Woking and Send. Subsequently he applied to licence Thornycroft J-type twenty-six-seat bus PP 1013 and another AEC B-type, LN 4760.

However, there was no sign of any activity commencing in Woking by the end of June 1924, so the council decided not to renew the licences. By May 1924 Weaver was trying to offload his Guildford operation to A & D but they were not prepared to pay his asking price of £2,500 for the vehicles. The Wonersh route was withdrawn by Autumn 1925 and the Slough-based interests ended around the same time.

Returning now to Mr Settle, by September 1924 he was quoting the address 201 Boundary Road, Woking, being that of Mr B. Martin, of which more follows. Settle had replaced the former Burton bus with a Ford, registered PD 6352. He used the fleet name 'Bus de Ville'. In December 1924 Messrs Spring, Didcock and Topp of Addlestone applied for permission to run a regular hourly service between Woking and Addlestone over Settle's route via Byfleet. This was to be operated by three fourteen-seat buses and would

As no photographs of buses belonging to Messrs Burton, Settle or Martin have been located, here is a view, possibly in Guildford, of two belonging to James Weaver's District Bus Service. Weaver applied for licences in Woking in 1923 but these were never used. The larger bus is PP 1013, a Thornycroft J type, while the other may be one of his Fords. (*Alan Lambert Collection*)

have provided significant competition for Settle. The council was minded to approve the service subject to the usual conditions, but it seems not to have reached fruition. Frank Topp had a grocery shop in Addlestone, while Spring, Didcock and Topp offered their business to A & D in June 1928, but the latter were not interested. Subsequently the business of J. W. Didcock of Chertsey, trading as the Reo Bus Service, whose services ran from Chertsey and Ottershaw to Walton on Thames via Addlestone and Weybridge, was acquired along with four vehicles by London Transport on 15 December 1933.

In June 1925 Settle acquired a second bus – another fourteen-seat Ford – to be used on his service although not at the same time as his other vehicle. Six round trips were operated. When an application by A. Leigh of Slough was made for a similar route in September 1925, it was declined. In December that year Settle applied for a second route between Woking and Chertsey but via Six Cross Roads and Woodham, joining the original route at New Haw (White Hart). W. Eggleton had already been granted a temporary licence for such a service.

Another person interested in linking Byfleet with Woking via New Haw and Woodham was Mr H. Howard of Howard's Garage, on the corner of Claremont Road and Station Avenue in West Byfleet. He applied unsuccessfully for a licence in May 1926. This operator is attributed with taking delivery of the very first example of the ubiquitous Duple-bodied Bedford – a twenty-seat bus of the WLB model that arrived in 1931. Registered MV 8996, it still survives. In the early 1930s, Howard had road service licences to run a round trip on Sunday afternoons from West Byfleet Station to St Martin's and St Nicholas's Homes in Pyrford, some sort of service on Mondays to Fridays from West Byfleet to Wisley, as well as special services as required to Byfleet and Pyrford village halls and to Byfleet and Weybridge Station on the occasions of Parish Day, dances, fêtes, concerts, whist drives and social functions.

In July 1926 Mr H. L. Medhurst was refused permission to operate between Pyrford and Woking on an hourly basis. Medhurst, of The Green, Pyrford, wanted to run via Maybury Inn, Shaftesbury Road and Heathside Road. He was supported by Reverend Cuthbert Hamilton, Vicar of Pyrford and Chairman of the Parish Council, who wanted to see a bus service provided for his village. Despite eventually gaining approval in November, the residents of the upmarket houses in the roads between Maybury Inn and Woking town centre were not happy, sending to the council a thirty-five-signature petition and nineteen letters addressed to councillors. In response, Medhurst offered to alter his route to run via Maybury Hill and Maybury Road, rather than serve an area where he was not likely to be patronised.

Settle applied in April 1927 for a service from Woking to Byfleet via Maybury Inn and Pyrford, which prompted the council to seek clarification from Medhurst as to whether he was actually going to start his service, which had been approved in principle five months earlier. By the following month Settle's address was recorded as Rivington, 40 Abbey Road, Horsell, although the occupier's name was given in a contemporary directory as Mrs D. Martin. He acquired a third bus – a twenty-seat Guy registered PH 2022. On 15 June the council formally revoked consent for Medhurst to operate and proposed to accede to Settle's request for a service via Pyrford which started by 1 August 1927.

However, by the end of September, Settle had withdrawn the Pyrford service in the morning as it was not found to be a paying proposition. He also complained that

Another operator who had designs on the Woking to Byfleet route (in 1926) was H. Howard of West Byfleet. Ford PD 4654 was perhaps employed on some sort of railway station shuttle service when seen here. (*J. Higham Collection/Alan Cross*)

A later Howard vehicle was MV 8996, a Bedford WLB said to be the very first chassis from this manufacturer to be bodied by Duple, in 1931. The Bedford/Duple combination was to become ubiquitous among the fleets of coach firms and many bus operators across the whole of the UK. (*J. Higham Collection/Alan Cross*)

Clifford Ross had started an unauthorised service on Sunday evenings between Woking and Maybury Inn, five minutes in front of his own service. The council asked Ross for an explanation and required that he discontinue such activity. Perhaps in retaliation, Settle unsuccessfully sought in November a number of additional Sunday journeys between Woking station and Maybury Inn. By the end of December 1927 the name of Bertram Henry Martin appeared in the council minutes in connection with Bus de Ville, in succession to Settle. The latter was of course previously acquainted with the Martin family by lodging with them or using their address, perhaps in order to be thought of as a locally based operator in the eyes of Woking Council, allowing him to potentially gain support over outside competitors. The Settle/Martin relationship remains unclear.

By January 1928, Martin was recorded as offering eleven round trips between Woking and Chertsey with some via Pyrford, so the latter was actually served by a diversion of the main Chertsey service. There were additional journeys between Woking and Byfleet on Saturdays and it was successfully proposed to extend some of these through to Chertsey. In April 1928 Martin renewed the application for additional Sunday journeys out to Maybury Inn. As A & D had applied to do the same, the council adjourned the matter until such time as both operators submitted timetables which did not clash with each other.

On 17 April 1929, one of Martin's buses, known as 'Dusty Bill' (Ford PD 6352 or PE 1419) caught fire and burnt out at West Weybridge (now Byfleet & New Haw) station. The vehicle was being driven by Henry Lagden and although Byfleet fire brigade was summoned, they declined to attend as the incident was just over the border in the Addlestone brigade's area. The latter eventually arrived in a car, equipped with only two fire extinguishers, by which time the bus had been completely destroyed. Martin acquired two further vehicles around May 1929, one of them being a fourteen-seat Chevrolet. In September 1930, licences were requested in the joint names of B. H. Martin and his wife Mrs O. Martin, only two buses being licensed by the end of that year. As well as using the 'Bus de Ville' name, the Martins also traded as The Red Bus.

With the enactment of the Road Traffic Act 1930 just over the horizon, there was a last flurry of speculative licence applications to establish services before the legislation came into force. Among these were those from Mr R. Thurston of Oyster Lane, Byfleet for a route from Weybridge to Woking via Byfleet and Maybury, and from W. H. Ross of 29 Downview Avenue, Westfield, for a short route from Woking station to Maybury via Walton Road. Needless to say, there were objections from established operators on the same roads, timings would clash and the Ccuncil considered these routes to be adequately served, hence the applications were declined in November 1930.

The East Surrey Traction Co. had been active in Woking since London General handed over to it some of the former Woking & District services of the Fox family in January 1931. No doubt keen to consolidate their position on the routes to the east of the town, they entered into negotiations with the Martins, who may have wished to leave the bus business before the start of the regulated regime. Mr Martin had a previous offer for his business from A & D in July 1930, when the £500 they offered was refused, but now Martin was ready to sell. His address was given as 41 Chertsey Road, Woking, when East Surrey made their purchase on 11 March 1931, retaining the Chevrolet and the Guy for around four months. They continued the Bus de Ville service, numbering it 40 (or 40A via Pyrford) on 20 May 1931, subsequent changes being recorded in the other chapters.

A. G. Smith

The First Woking Acquisition by 'The Tracco'

The first reference to the activities of Arthur G. Smith appears in the local press in September 1921, by way of an advertisement for an early morning bus service from Knaphill (Garibaldi P. H.), leaving at 6.15 a.m. via St Johns and Woking station to Weybridge station. At the latter, a connection could be made for a 'work-men's' train to Waterloo – perhaps this offered a cheaper way of reaching London than catching a train from Woking. Possibly the same person, an Arthur George Smith was a nurseryman by 1913 in Robin Hood Road but there is no reference to that activity in the 1918 directory.

Smith, who lived at The Bungalow, Anchor Hill, Lower Knaphill, probably utilised his bus for the rest of the day on, predictably, the Knaphill–St Johns–Woking route, his fourteen-seat Ford vehicle registered PC 5710 being licensed by Woking Council in October 1921. He also applied for a driver's licence for daughter Miss N. Smith, which caused some fluttering at the Highways Committee. Councillor Heather asked whether it was right to grant a licence to a young girl when many men were unemployed. The chairman responded that the council could not refuse the application if she was physically fit and technically able, to which Lady Betty Balfour said 'hear, hear!' Lady Balfour was the first female elected member on Woking Council from 1919 and represented the St Johns ward. Councillor Heather's view struck a chord with a man who had a letter published in the *Woking News & Mail*, challenging the decision on the licence when there were 700 unemployed men in the town, adding that 'it was quite all right when the war was on. The sooner the Female Set devote their energy to the occupation most fitted for them, namely domestic service, the sooner we shall emerge out of our present industrial chaos.' Views like that were quite common at that time.

By May 1922, Smith had acquired another small bus and a twenty-seat Ford charabanc, with trips in it being advertised. The morning bus to Weybridge was still running (6 a.m. from Knaphill, fare two shillings) and Smith was running from Knaphill to Woking via both St Johns and Horsell. In due course, Smith started running from Woking to Chobham via Horsell, after which the Knaphill service probably only ran via St Johns. He also ran beyond Knaphill to Bisley and West End. The two service buses were replaced in January 1923 by two new fourteen-seat Fords, later being supplemented by a fourteen-seat Overland. In September 1923, a wheel came off one of the buses in Horsell while on the way from West End to Woking – the passengers 'escaped with a shaking'.

By June 1924 Smith was making fifteen journeys each way between Knaphill and Woking. At that time he attempted to gain a place on the Woking to Send route via Old Woking but the council viewed this unfavourably, finding it neither necessary or desirable for another operator to be on that route. From July, it appears he abandoned Bisley and West End, perhaps in the face of competition from A & D's service 34 and instead extended his route beyond Knaphill to Brookwood, Pirbright Camp, Deepcut Camp, Blackdown Camp and Frimley Green. In October 1924 this was extended again, as far as Frimley station, at which time Smith had six vehicles in his Blue Omnibus fleet – three Fords, the Overland, a Fiat and a GMC. The following month the Frimley service was extended to Yorktown and Camberley. Conversely, Smith withdrew from Chobham, possibly from early 1925 when Stanley Tanner gained a licence for the route.

Smith took one of his drivers to court in May 1925 with a £5 claim for damages. Alfred Jukes was a driver and mechanic who lived away from home and was paid £3 per week. When Jukes' wife visited Woking to see him, he wanted her to travel on his bus while in service. Smith would not permit that so Jukes left without giving notice. At the hearing it emerged that the real reason he was dissatisfied was that he felt he could not drive a bus with poor brakes and a damaged chassis. On being fined £2, he suggested that Smith should pay him damages for his clothes spoilt by his dirty vehicles.

Woking Council's recently appointed hackney carriage inspector noted in June 1925 that Smith (three buses) as well as Fox (seven buses) had been running a shuttle service to Pirbright, Blackdown and Deepcut Camps, following the arrival of two Sunday evening trains from London at Brookwood station. Each train disgorged between 200 and 300 servicemen returning from weekend leave and many of these were quickly transported by the waiting buses, which the local police sergeant found most helpful for clearing the streets, despite strong protest from taxi proprietors. These journeys ran after the normal bus service had ended for the day. It was also reported that six to ten buses waited outside Highclere Hall in Knaphill between 10.30 and 11 p.m. on certain days, to convey both civilian and military passengers to various places at the conclusion of social functions held there. This operation was also welcomed by the police and the request that these two special facilities should be continued was granted by the council.

Smith's son William was taken to court for the alleged dangerous driving of a coach at Knaphill High Street at 10.45 p.m. on 4 July 1925. He was in Fiat PD 1174 and a police constable stated that he had been driving it at 20–25 mph in a dangerous fashion. As there was some discrepancy in witness statements, William was fined £4 for speeding but escaped prosecution for dangerous driving. Another incident involving him was to occur the following month when he accidentally knocked down William Kurn in Guildford Road, Knaphill. Kurn had been drinking in Knaphill Working Mens' Club and apparently was oblivious to the approaching bus. William took Kurn in his bus to Woking Hospital but the latter died there next day. A verdict of misadventure was recorded and Smith was totally exonerated.

By Summer 1925, the Camberley route had been considerably shortened to terminate at Blackdown Post Office. However, Arthur Smith's business suffered a severe setback in the early hours of Saturday morning, 3 October 1925. He was visiting a son at Downe in Kent, although his other two sons, William and Tommy were at home at The Bungalow. Shortly after 1 a.m. they were woken by the furious barking of dogs, to find

Although of poor quality (a proper print was not available), this photograph does provide a rare illustration of one of Arthur Smith's buses. One of his Ford Ts has been decorated for some event although the posing couple have not been identified. (*Peter Holmes Collection*)

Smith had taken delivery of this charabanc with removable canvas roof by spring 1924. PD 1174 was a Fiat, quite likely bodied in Woking by F. W. Coulter. Used on bus services as well as coaching work, it was destroyed in the fire at Smith's garage, but not before William Smith had received a speeding fine for driving it too fast through Knaphill! (*Alan Lambert Collection*)

Following the fire at Smith's garage in October 1925, replacement vehicles had to be obtained. Two Republic twenty-seaters with bodywork by Coulter soon arrived, the second being PE 7415, photographed carrying tentative 'Saloon Coach Service' sign-writing. (*Alan Lambert Collection*)

the bus garage on fire and flames shooting high into the air. One of the dogs was chained to a tree in the yard and had frantically dug a hole in which it was trying to bury itself in terror of the fire. Fortunately, the garage was some way from the house but igniting petrol tanks on the vehicles caused the galvanised iron garage roof to fall in and the heat was intense, but two petrol pumps, underground tanks and forty gallons of motor oil escaped the conflagration. Tommy ran half a mile in his bare feet to summon the Knaphill fire brigade. The latter suffered confusion, their first impression being that the fire was at Brookwood. By the time they got to Knaphill, they were unable to save the garage or its contents. The chief officer of the Woking brigade advised that in the future, those reporting fires should directly telephone Woking fire station, clearly indicating where the fire was.

Arthur Smith was summoned back from Kent and arrived to find that his two Fords, the Fiat and the GMC had been destroyed, along with an Armstrong-Siddeley car used as a taxi. The heat had been so intense that glass had fused and metalwork had twisted, including aluminium engine casings that had melted. The only remaining parts left of one engine were the bearings. Smith had bought the GMC for £1,000 and had just spent £25 in having it repainted. He was booked to take a large party to Wembley the following week and had been left with just one bus (the Overland) for his regular service. This escaped the fire as he had used it for his trip to Kent. The cause of the fire was unknown.

Arthur Smith's predicament meant that fewer journeys could be provided between Woking and Knaphill in the short term, however, being suitably insured, he had the garage rebuilt and purchased two new buses. These were on Republic chassis, with twenty-seat bodywork built locally in Woking by F. W. Coulter under the 'Perfecta' brand name. The first was in service by the end of October and the second by mid-November 1925. Meanwhile, the competitive animosity between the various small firms on the Woking–Knaphill route continued, at a time that A & D was also expanding its offering over that road. From time to time, Smith had come in for criticism regarding irregular operation and practices while he in turn was quick to report to the council the misdemeanours of others. On the road, tempers sometimes became frayed and on 1 April 1926 there was a dispute leading to a fight between one of Smith's drivers and of one of Fox's Woking & District employees.

A & D realised that as far as the Woking area was concerned, the best way of consolidating or expanding its position was to acquire the businesses of small local operators. This process got underway in April 1926 when negotiations were opened with Arthur Smith, who had approached A & D the previous month. Agreement was eventually reached so that on 9 June 1926, A & D took over the Woking–Blackdown service (numbering it 28B), and the two Republic vehicles and the Overland, for which they paid £2,250. They also purchased shortly afterwards Smith's garage at Knaphill for £1,200, this being the first time that A & D could keep buses under cover in the Woking area. Smith himself moved to Horsell but was probably gone by 1931.

London General,
East Surrey & Green Line

Belatedly Closing the Circle

The London General Omnibus Co. Ltd gradually embraced the motor bus in the first decade of the twentieth century, manufacturing its own vehicles including the famous B-type, introduced in 1910 as a great step forward in bus design. The Underground Electric Railways Company of London Ltd (UERL) in 1912 took over London General. This grouping became known as the London Traffic Combine and became an unstoppable force in London's public transport. From UERL, London General inherited Albert Stanley (later Lord Ashfield) as managing director and Frank Pick, in charge of the Traffic, Development and Advertising Department. It is probably fair to say that the combined differing talents of these two men made the Underground Group and later London Transport the leading provider of modern urban transport, evolving a unique, ground-breaking style in all that it did. Many aspects of the Underground Group, or 'Combine', have been comprehensively covered elsewhere in numerous books.

Unsurprisingly, General's far-reaching ambitions for service development were thwarted by the First World War and for two to three years afterwards. Like A & D, General struggled after the war to rebuild its business and although it ran out into Surrey (the county was larger then), there were still plenty of areas ripe for bus service development. The opening of a new bus garage in Kingston on 4 January 1922 was the springboard for the further expansion into Surrey and south Middlesex. Operated by the twenty-six seat single-deck model of the AEC B-type, General had a service 79 from Kingston to Esher and Cobham, which was extended to Byfleet and West Byfleet from 29 June 1921. Shortly after that, on 27 July 1921, General started a service 112 from Kingston to Weybridge station via Esher and Hersham; on the day the new garage opened, this was extended to Byfleet, West Byfleet, Maybury Inn, Old Woking, Kingfield Green and Woking, taking the 79 number and operating hourly. Cobham was then left to service 115 from Kingston to Guildford.

As early as April 1921, General was advising Woking Council that they wished to extend the original service 79 from Cobham to Woking. The company asked for their comments about the route to be followed and applied for licences for ten buses. An hourly weekday facility and a half-hourly Sunday service were envisaged to start in late May. However, the council was concerned about the extra wear and tear on local roads and enquired whether General would pay something towards their upkeep. There was a suggestion that the Byfleet to Woking road would need strengthening and

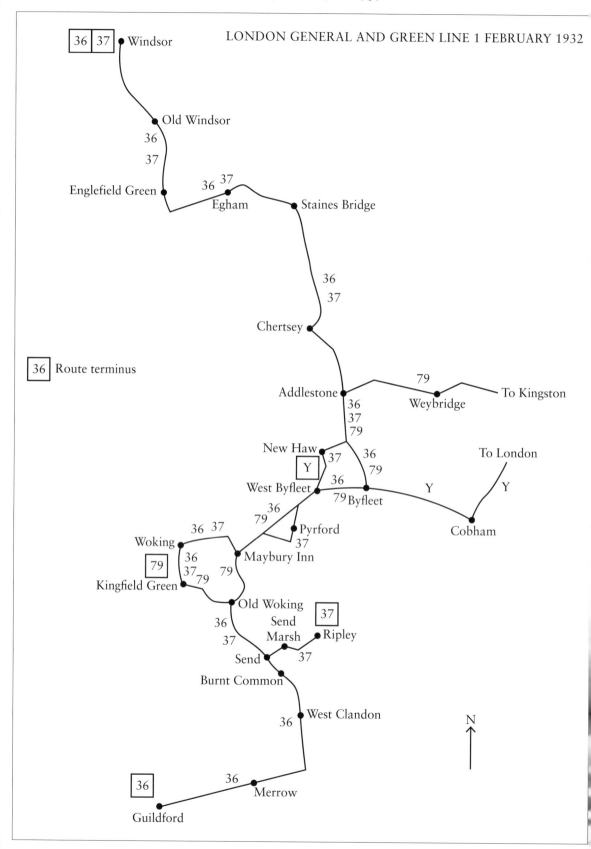

LONDON GENERAL AND GREEN LINE 1 FEBRUARY 1932

36 37 ● Windsor

● Old Windsor

36
37

Englefield Green ●

36 37
Egham ●

● Staines Bridge

36
37

Chertsey ●

36 Route terminus

79
Addlestone ● — ● To Kingston
36 Weybridge
37
79

New Haw ●
Y
37 36
West Byfleet ● 79
36 Y Y
79 Byfleet
36 To London
79
Cobham ●

36 ● Pyrford
Woking ● 79
36 37 37
36 Maybury Inn
79 Y 79
37 79
Kingfield Green ●

● Old Woking
36 Send 37
37 Marsh ● Ripley
Send ● 37
Burnt Common ●

36 ● West Clandon

N
↑

36
36 ●
Merrow
36 ●
Guildford

widening and mixed views on the proposed new service, which would bring benefit to the local economy, but 'would it disturb the calm of peoples' Sundays' by bringing hordes of Londoners for a day in the countryside? General pointed out that they were already paying increased road fund duty as a contribution to highway maintenance and, being unable to make a direct local contribution, suggested that the council apply to the Ministry of Transport for assistance. Chertsey Rural District Council was also concerned, advising General that the Byfleet to Woking road was 'not safe for the proposed bus route and the road crust was not of sufficient thickness at present'.

The Woking branch of the Amalgamated Engineering Union passed a resolution protesting against the action of the council in not granting licences, while a letter of support from a resident to the *Woking News & Mail* cynically commented, 'tis sad to be awakened from one's slumber at, say, 10 a.m. by wicked people who prefer to enjoy a life of activity to that of a wounded hermit. The Nobility of Woking are objecting to the common herd who do not have Rolls Royces or Fords.' To move matters forward, Woking Council asked Surrey County Council to reclassify the Byfleet to Woking road, but they were unable to assist. However, in early July 1921 the ten bus licences were granted but still no service commenced as, possibly due to frustration over the delay, General had postponed their plans.

Later in 1922 the B-type vehicles were replaced with the new thirty-seat AEC 401 S-type. Initially the whole service was operated by Kingston garage, but on 16 May 1923 General opened a small garage in Thames Street, Weybridge. This provided eight buses for several local services, including the 79, out-stationed from Kingston. In September 1924 and again in 1925, General wrote to Woking Council asking permission to use double-deckers but this was refused as the surveyor still thought the route quite unsuitable for such vehicles. By the end of 1925 General was also using some of their AEC K-type single-deckers to supplement the S-type.

In spring 1926 General were contemplating a fifteen-minute-interval Sunday and Bank Holiday service aimed at leisure traffic, all the way from Feltham in Middlesex and approaching Woking from the Chertsey direction via Ottershaw. The council suggested a thirty-minute-interval service, which should be timed so as not to clash with the Woking–Chertsey service of Clifford Ross, but in the event, General did not take the idea further.

Service 79 was diverted from 25 May 1927 away from Caenswood Hill past Brooklands Racing Circuit, so as to run between Weybridge and Byfleet via Addlestone, New Haw (White Hart) and West Weybridge station, bringing some competition for Settle's Chertsey–Byfleet–Woking service. Another tentative service proposal from General, unfulfilled for the time being, came in October 1927 when an hourly service was put forward to run between Guildford and Woking via Burpham, Send and Old Woking.

The East Surrey Traction Co. Ltd was founded in Reigate in 1911, principally by Arthur Henry Hawkins. Under his energetic direction, business acumen and ruthless techniques when dealing with local competition, the company expanded to cover much of south and east Surrey and parts of northern Sussex. Before the First World War, London General ran few services beyond the immediate built-up area of London as existed at that time, but as early as 1914 a significant boundary agreement was made between

London General opened this garage in Thames Street, Weybridge in 1923. It provided some of the buses for service 79 from Kingston to Woking and closed in late 1939 under London Transport auspices. (*London Transport Museum*)

General and East Surrey. The boundary was broadly established as the road at the foot of the North Downs (later to become the A25) from Guildford, through to Sevenoaks, although both companies had permission to cross this line under specified circumstances. The shortages of vehicles and men caused by the war prevented General doing much to extend its empire southwards. However, by 1919, Hawkins was seeking a closer working relationship with General, being on good terms with Lord Ashfield and Frank Pick. He could see that partnership would be more productive than painful competition and was concerned that the area between the Metropolitan Police boundary and the A25 might pose a threat to his company if other significant operators became established there.

Therefore, another agreement dated 7 July 1921 defined three areas of operation as 'The London Area', 'The London Country Area' and 'The Traction Company's Area'. In the London Country Area and across the boundary into The London Area, East Surrey was given the right to operate bus services on behalf of London General. It could also develop 'joint' services from its own area into the London Country Area. London General undertook to provide East Surrey the necessary buses and garages needed for services operated on its behalf. East Surrey apparently intended to run in the Woking area as early as December 1923, when they proposed a service from Horsell to Chertsey.

When East Surrey wrote to Woking Council in April 1928, advising of their plan for a joint route with A & D at half-hourly intervals from Guildford to Chertsey via Woking, New Haw and Addlestone, it was probably with the consent of London General under the terms of the 'agency' agreement. In view of the many other bus services operating

From 1926, London General was supplementing the S-type buses on service 79 to Woking with some examples of the similar K-type, represented here by K605 (XC 8292) on 28 July 1929. The last Ks were withdrawn by the end of 1931. (*W. Noel Jackson/Alan Cross*)

over parts of this route in their area, particularly that of Woking & District between Send and Woking, the council refused to grant licences. Three months later, General themselves tried a different approach when they proposed to divert their service 171 (Kingston-Chertsey) at Addlestone to run to Woodham, Woking, Send and Guildford. This was also refused although Guildford Council had no objections, nor did they when Woking & District extended their Woking–Send service to West Clandon, Merrow and Guildford in about September 1928. After this frustration, East Surrey awarded themselves consolation with an hourly service 31 from Guildford as far as Send, via Merrow and West Clandon from 31 October 1928. Worked with a fourteen-seat Guy vehicle based at Leatherhead garage, it only lasted until 15 April 1930 and in the meantime General tried again in March 1929, without success, to extend service 171, while East Surrey tried again to extend service 31 to Woking and Chertsey in September 1929.

During 1928 the four main railway companies had been granted statutory powers to operate their own bus services, but instead began to buy up substantial holdings in existing bus companies. One could have expected the Southern Railway to invest in East Surrey, which concerned General, who saw their southern boundary threatened. After negotiations between Frank Pick and Arthur Hawkins, the Underground Group acquired a controlling interest in East Surrey by an agreement of 23 May 1929. East Surrey Traction Co. Ltd became a subsidiary of the London General Omnibus Co. Ltd. The buses that East Surrey had operated on loan from General were largely in the latter's red and white livery but with East Surrey fleet names, and the takeover by General was signalled by a decision to change East Surrey's own livery from royal blue and white to General's red.

With the advancement of vehicle design and reliability, new and better roads and pneumatic tyres, the second half of the 1920s saw a rapid proliferation of longer-distance limited-stop coach services into central London from outlying suburban areas and the so-called country districts in the surrounding Home Counties. Both East Surrey and General had started such services. However, many of the services were developed by independent operators, and one of these was Charles Dobbs's Skylark Motor Coach Co. Ltd, based at Ledbury Mews, North Kensington, London W11. They started a frequent Guildford to London service on 17 December 1928, via Ripley, Cobham and Esher and by spring 1929 were applying to operate hourly journeys via Mayford, Woking and Byfleet as well. The Through Omnibus Services Joint Advisory Committee recommended refusal on the grounds that the service was not necessary in the public interest, especially as there was at least three fast trains per hour between Woking and London. Skylark was persistent and appealed to the Minister of Transport. An inquiry was held at Woking in December 1929 when the council showed its reluctance to licence any more buses and coaches on the grounds of town centre congestion and that Woking was already well served. In January 1930 it was announced that Skylark's appeal against the decision had failed. Meanwhile, in late 1929 Woking Council had adjourned applications for Woking–London services by various routes from F. A. Reynolds, Highways Ltd, Premier Omnibus Co. Ltd and Blue Belle Motors Ltd, pending the outcome of the Skylark appeal, after which they were also refused. In July 1930, Skylark's solicitor tried again for licences in Woking, again without success. This was James Cort Bathurst, a formidable legal advocate who worked, usually successfully, to represent the interests of many small bus and coach companies in the London area.

To create an identity for their new coach services, with a livery different to the red colour scheme normally employed on buses, General created a new subsidiary on 9 July 1930 – Green Line Coaches Ltd. Thus, a famous brand was born and the company embarked on an ambitious programme of expansion and acquisition. In October 1930 this new company sought a coach service from Guildford to Windsor via Woking, but this was refused on the grounds that the existing services adequately served the needs of Woking in respect of those destinations. Skylark was eventually acquired by Green Line on 6 February 1932, together with its fleet of Gilford coaches in a dark green livery, although the Skylark company temporarily survived as a subsidiary.

The Underground Group's aspiration was to expand outwards to form a comprehensive network in the suburbs and country areas surrounding London, although as has been seen, with little success in the Woking area. Up to the end of 1930, there was only service 79. There was an impending deadline of 9 February 1931 – the last day on which a new service could be started that would be allowed to continue after 1 April 1931, when the Road Traffic Act came into force. With small likelihood of gaining licences from local authorities in time, General had to move fast if it was going to close the circle properly.

As already described, A & D started negotiating with the Fox family to purchase Woking & District in 1930 and invited London General to participate as the services ran both to the east and west of Woking, compromising the September 1927 boundary agreement between A & D, General and East Surrey. The tripartite purchase agreement between the companies saw the larger part of the Fox business immediately resold to General, including the garage at St Johns, four services and fifteen buses. These were Daimlers PD 6984, 8642 and 9993, Thornycrofts PF 7317, 7461, OT 7822, VB 4550, PG 1099, 1757, 1768, 2018, 3236 and 4226, Tilling Stevens PG 9381 and A. J. S. PG 9385. The purchase was completed on 14 January 1931 with General immediately handing over responsibility to its East Surrey subsidiary. Woking Council eventually agreed to transfer licences from Fox to East Surrey, although originally it had stated that it would only transfer them to A & D as an established local operator.

The four services were Woking–Old Woking–Send–West Clandon–Merrow–Guildford; Woking–Old Woking–Send–Ripley; Woking–Ottershaw–Chertsey–Staines Bridge–Egham–Englefield Green–Windsor; and West Byfleet–New Haw–Addlestone–Ottershaw–Chertsey–Staines Bridge–Egham–Englefield Green–Windsor. For some months East Surrey purely perpetuated Fox's timetables and routes, using the Woking

& District vehicles in their original livery. Only the revised legal ownership details on the vehicles gave an indication that part of W & D had been acquired by the Combine. However, Thornycrofts PF 7317 and 7461 were withdrawn and replaced by two of East Surrey's own vehicles. From 20 May 1931, the aforementioned services were numbered 36–39 respectively. Each service operated hourly on a daily basis, nine buses being needed, although there was a need for extras on Saturday afternoons and evenings, when two additional journeys per hour were run on service 36 between Woking and Old Woking and on service 38 between Chertsey and Staines.

Meanwhile, there were developments involving Green Line Coaches. Just ahead of the 9 February deadline, a new daily service was introduced on 31 January 1931 to London (the new Poland Street Coach Station near Oxford Circus) every half-hour from West Byfleet via Byfleet, Cobham, Esher, Hinchley Wood, Tolworth, Roehampton, Barnes and Hammersmith. Naturally enough, it was originally intended to start this service from Woking, running to West Byfleet via Old Woking and Maybury Inn (along the route of service 79) but Woking Council would not grant licences. The service was operated by six of the new AEC Regal coaches of the T class, in the chosen Green Line livery of dark green and black. These were based at the Weymann's bus building premises in Station Road, Addlestone and worked in service to/from Byfleet via New Haw. On 21 February the service was designated as Y in a new lettering scheme used to identify the Green line routes, and responsibility for the Addlestone garaging arrangements passed from General to East Surrey control. When an application was submitted for a road service licence under the Road Traffic Act, it was intended that alternate coaches would proceed onwards from Esher to Woking via Cobham and Byfleet or via Hersham, Weybridge and Byfleet, each running hourly. These additions to service Y were refused by the traffic commissioner and as far as the western end of the route was concerned, East Surrey ended up with just a service to West Byfleet via Cobham again.

The initial 'country' bus network east of Woking was completed on 11 March 1931, when East Surrey acquired the Bus de Ville business of Bertram Martin with his route from Woking to Chertsey via Byfleet and Addlestone. This was numbered 40 on 20 May, when it was basically a daily hourly service, but alternate trips on Sunday to Friday afternoons ran as 40A via Pyrford, which additionally worked every hour on Saturday afternoons and evenings between Woking and Byfleet only. Two buses were required and three on Saturdays. When East Surrey applied for licences from the traffic commissioner for their services in July 1931, they proposed to divert services 40/40A between Woking and Maybury Inn via Kingfield Green and Old Woking but this was refused.

On 31 May 1931 the former Woking & District garage at St Johns was closed and was replaced by a building in Walton Road, Woking, just vacated by A & D. East Surrey rented the Walton Road premises, where fifteen buses were allocated for services 36–40. In June 1927, General had bought land at Mays Corner, Send, where it would build a garage for sixteen vehicles. Agreement in principle from Surrey County Council had been secured in November 1927. Then, new planning regulations resulted in the land being zoned for residential purposes and a planning application was refused by Guildford Rural District Council in November 1928. An inquiry held in The Drill Hall, Send in February1931 brought forth numerous objections from local residents who thought the proposed garage would devalue their property, although General maintained their need for it as twenty Green Line coaches were in temporary accommodation at Addlestone and twelve on open land at Rice & Harper's premises in Guildford. However, the availability of the Walton Road facility in Woking resulted in the Send project not being pursued. In June 1931 two new Morris Viceroy buses were sent to Woking by East Surrey as spares for the former Fox vehicles. These were later replaced by one ADC 416-type with open cab and tarpaulin for protection of the driver in bad weather. This was a poor substitute for the two Morris Viceroys, thus the number of former Fox vehicles failed with defects took a noticeable fall.

General replaced the S-type buses on service 79 with AEC Regal T-types in August 1931. Although numbered in the T series (1000–1002) there were also three experimental buses manufactured by the company itself at their Chiswick Works, and these spent their entire lives allocated to Kingston and Weybridge, being used on services including the 79/219 until February 1938.

In late 1931 it was proposed to transfer to East Surrey Traction Co. those joint services north of London which were operated on behalf of London General by National Omnibus & Transport Co. Ltd. This involved operations in Middlesex, Hertfordshire, Buckinghamshire and Essex, so the name of East Surrey was no longer appropriate. Therefore, on 28 January 1932 the company was renamed London General Country Services Ltd (LGCS). The standard bus livery of red, white and black was retained with a General Country Services fleet name. However, around May 1933 vehicles emerging from overhaul were painted green and black as an initial move towards giving the 'country' area operations a separate identity.

Although East Surrey were running between Woking and Maybury Inn via Maybury Road after acquiring Martin's service, A & D regarded this as 'their road' after acquiring Ross's service in January 1928. A & D were to encourage East Surrey to withdraw but, planning for the setting up of London Transport, focussed on the opposite when it was decided that Maybury should fall in the latter's new territory. This event was pre-empted on 1 February 1932, when LGCS revised their local services and A & D acquired from LGCS sole rights to operate from Woking to Chertsey via Ottershaw. This had been allowed for in the purchase agreement for the Woking & District business, and resulted in the demise of LGCS service 38.

Of the former W & D services, the hourly 36, was extended from Woking to Maybury Inn, West Byfleet, Byfleet, New Haw, Addlestone, Chertsey, Staines Bridge, Egham, Englefield Green, Old Windsor and Windsor, while the hourly 37 was extended in much the same way. However, the 37 also covered Pyrford and ran between West Byfleet and New Haw (White Hart) via Scotland Bridge Road and Woodham Lane, part of New Haw that London Transport later referred to as Woodham. This in turn allowed the withdrawal of services 38, 39 and 40/40A. The associated reduction in the overall level of service between Woking and Maybury Inn was not popular with local residents. As part of the transfer of responsibility, A & D Dennis 4-ton single-decker PH 1106 was transferred to LGCS in December 1932, although the question of compensation for A & D in respect of losing the Maybury Inn route was not settled until after the formation of London Transport.

The rented premises for Green Line Coaches at the Weymann factory in Addlestone were replaced in November 1932 by facilities (also rented) at the former premises of

One of Woking & District's Thornycroft BCs, PG 1758, seen soon after acquisition by East Surrey. It is on the Woking to Guildford service, which was numbered 36, although not visibly labelled as such on this vehicle. (*Alan Lambert Collection*)

Thornycroft A2L PG 4226 still carries the Woking & District livery and fleet name when seen soon after takeover by East Surrey, but note the new legal ownership panel. Just visible on the right is a Leyland TD1 double-decker of Thames Valley, so the location may well be Windsor, with the Thornycroft heading for West Byfleet on what was to become service 39. (*N. Hamshere Collection*)

PG 9381 was the only Fox Tilling-Stevens of 1930 to pass to East Surrey, the other three going to A&D. When photographed, East Surrey had been renamed London General Country Services but the bus was still working in the Woking area. The view dates from after February 1932, when service 36 had been extended to run all the way from Windsor to Guildford. (*J. Higham Collection/Alan Cross*)

Also seen working on service 36 is PH 8883, an Associated Daimler (ADC) 426 with Short Bros. thirty-seat rear entrance bodywork. New to East Surrey in 1928, it originally had twenty-eight coach seats. (*J. Higham Collection/Alan Cross*)

To replace the former Fox premises at St Johns, East Surrey rented this garage in Walton Road, Woking in 1931, after use by A&D. In May 1933 the vehicle allocation was moved to Hamm Moor Lane at Weybridge. Note the adjacent Billiards Hall, no doubt popular with bus staff when off-duty. (*London Transport Museum*)

Hoyal, a bus body builder, in Hamm Moor Lane on what is now the Weybridge Trading Estate.

In January 1933, Green Line was still appealing to the Minister of Transport over the decision of the south-eastern traffic commissioner not to allow service Y to run through to Woking due to insufficient evidence of need, although the extension had been approved by the Metropolitan traffic commissioner. He seemed to be protecting the railway company, who admitted that they had lost patronage on suburban routes in other areas where Green Line ran. In any case, the appeal was unsuccessful and service Y continued only as far as West Byfleet for the time being.

In September 1930, Herbert Morrison, the Minister of Transport in the Labour government, announced his intentions to create a single statutory public transport entity for London and surrounding areas, which would unify the companies of the Underground Group Combine, Metropolitan Railway, the municipal tramway systems, and all other bus companies. A Bill was published on 13 March 1931 with provisions to give the new London Passenger Transport Board a monopoly within its defined area, which roughly aligned with the sphere of influence of London General and its subsidiaries. The statutory boundary formed a ring around London, passing through Horsham, Guildford, Woking and Egham. Much of the area within this boundary would

Although numbered as part of the T class for convenience, T1000–1002 were not AEC Regals: they were experimental vehicles built by London General itself at Chiswick Works in 1931 and were easily recognised by their elongated bonnets and unusual radiator design. This is T1001 (GT 7446), which spent much of its life on service 79, later 219, from Weybridge and Kingston garages. (J. Higham Collection/Alan Cross)

be a monopoly, named 'The Special Area', which extended right up to the traditional boundary with A & D through the middle of Woking. No other bus company could operate within the 'Special Area' without specific permission from the board and powers were included to enable acquisition of existing small companies then running in the same area. Under a new national government, the Bill continued its progress and received Royal Assent on 13 April 1933. The London Passenger Transport Act was effective from 1 July that year – a momentous date for public transport integration in London. This spelt the end of the London General Omnibus Co. Ltd and subsidiary companies, and subsequent local events are dealt with in a later chapter.

W. S. Hunt

A Family Firm Still in Business

The first licensed passenger transport north-east from Woking along the direct road towards Chertsey seems to have been inaugurated by W. S. Hunt, who developed various motor-related activities at Richflower Garage, 71 Brox Road, Ottershaw. William Stanley Hunt moved to Ottershaw in 1915 with his wife Margaret to pursue his cocker spaniel and golden retriever dog breeding business, also being an international dog show judge. His dogs were exported widely and were much admired – indeed one customer in America named his farm as Ottershaw Farm. Hunt also supplied dog travelling boxes, kennels, food, straw and sawdust and claimed to be the sole manufacturer of products for dogs called 'Richflower' and 'Disper'. His letterhead had photographs of two prize dogs including 'Ottershaw Pimpernel', the best red cocker spaniel at Crufts in about 1929, as well as a view of Mr Hunt judging bulldogs in Melbourne, Australia.

Hunt is reputed to have been the first person in the village to own a car. He was to expand his business interest into a number of areas, including taxi and charabanc proprietor, haulage contractor and coal merchant. The premises in Brox Road expanded in 1923 when a barn on some land purchased from Fletcher Bros, previously part of Brox Farm, was converted into an office. William Hunt's daughter Lavinia remembers driving twenty- and twenty-five-seat Bedford coaches in the 1930s. She also remembers a party going to the Aldershot Tattoo on a lorry fitted with a canvas hood and a bench seat along each side.

In February 1922 Hunt had applied to run a service from Woking to Ottershaw via Maybury Road, Six Cross Roads and Bleak House, the latter a public house. The vehicle was a seven-seater of some sort, registered PB 6858, that was licensed by Chertsey Urban District Council in whose area Ottershaw was situated. During 1923 Clifford Ross started a service along a similar route to Hunt, running beyond Ottershaw to Chertsey. This seems to have resulted in a situation whereby, in June 1924, Woking Council had the understanding that Mr Hunt would probably not apply to renew his licence and there is no further reference to his bus service after that date.

Later circumstances give a convenient opportunity to include here some references to a Woking-based coach proprietor who did not run local bus services. As early as March 1914, Mr Conway West, originally described as a blacksmith from Mayford, ran a motor engineering works and sold petrol at his garage at 165 High Street, Old Woking. He traded as the Conway Cycle and Motor Agency. Once the war was over, people again felt able to consider the lighter side of life, such as a day trip to the seaside. In summer 1919 Conway Motor Works were advertising charabanc excursions to Bognor and Brighton, leaving at 7 a.m. for the sum of ten shillings – a fair amount for the working man in those days. Two motor vehicles were licensed by Woking Council. These were stated in May 1920 as being registered PA 9692 (named *Woking Conway*) and DB 1846, named *Woking Pearl*.

By June 1922 West had doubled his fleet to four charabancs and on 22 August that year he opened a magnificent petrol station (The Conway Petrol and Oil Service) on the junction of Victoria Road, Guildford Road and Railway Approach in Woking, with six petrol pumps. This was followed by the expansion of the Old Woking premises in April 1923, after the acquisition of adjacent land and buildings at the Albion Hotel Yard from the brewery firm Lascelles, Tickner & Co. Ltd. However, West sold the Old Woking premises to Mr A. Fleming in 1931. Conway West Motors Ltd was registered on 8 December 1926 and by 1930 seven coaches and five cars were operated. Captain G. C. Ritchie and A. H. Grubb became directors of the firm, in addition to Conway West. Further expansion occurred in April 1928 when Conway West Motors opened a new garage with car showrooms and filling station in Guildford Road, Woking.

Following the acquisition by Conway West of W. S. Hunt's Coaches Ltd (incorporated 31 March 1949), the operating base was moved to Ottershaw. The combined operation was renamed Conway Hunt Ltd on 22 March 1957 and undertook private hire, contracts, excursions and seasonal express coach services to the South Coast from points in Surrey and south-west London, under the control of Conway West's son Geoffrey. In 1959 Conway Hunt acquired Mears Motors Ltd of Richmond and in 1971 Kingston Luxury Coaches Ltd became an associated firm. In December 1975 some excursion licences for pick-ups in the Woking, Addlestone, Byfleet and Chertsey areas were sold to Safeguard Coaches of Guildford, together with two vehicles. Until the early 1970s, Conway Hunt had regularly purchased new coaches and for front-line work kept the fleet modern, in a smart yellow and grey livery. However, after that time, operations began to be scaled down. Following a transfer of the business to Monument Way West in Woking, Conway Hunt finally ceased operating in Summer 1985.

After the formation of Conway Hunt, the Hunt family continued in business at Ottershaw and were involved with road haulage and commercial vehicle repairs. William Hunt had two sons and two daughters, and it was son Bernard who diversified after the last war into the supply of petrol, diesel and heating oil. W. S. Hunt's Transport Ltd continues to operate a modern fleet of trucks, and contract hire and vehicle repairs are undertaken. The current directors are Malcolm Hunt and George Truett, grandsons of the founder William Hunt, and the fourth generation of the family also takes an active role.

Opposite: Another view of Brasier CT 351. Unfortunately, none of the assembled men and boys in this photograph can be identified, although the busman on the left is the same as in the photograph of Napier PB 8935 featured earlier. The common denominator between the two vehicles could have been John Denyer, so perhaps it is him or his driver. (*Iain Wakeford Collection*)

J. Denyer

Fried Fish and Bus

With the demise of Frank Mills' business, a gap in the market was duly identified by the likes of the Fox family and certain others who were tempted to enter the competitive fray on the St Johns to Woking route. One of these was John Denyer, a fried fish salesman from St Johns Road in 1911, who attended the auction at Mills' garage on 8 June 1921. He was interested in Mills' eight-seat Brasier bus (CT 351), which had last been licensed to V. B. Jenner.

He successfully, in his view, bid £22 10s for it and wrote out a cheque. However, he was told next day by the auctioneers, S. Atherton & Co. of Broadway, Woking that the bus had not been sold to him. Denyer took Athertons to court in November 1921 where he claimed either the bus or £100 from them. During the hearing it emerged that the sale book had been altered to £25 and that the bus had been 'bought in'. Sidney Stedman, described as a motor engineer from Woking, had apparently subsequently offered £40 for it.

Denyer insisted that he heard the auctioneer say 'yours – Denyer' and the hammer fell. In support, Ruby Mills said she heard £22 10s mentioned and wrote it down at the time. Judgement came on 1 December 1921 when Denyer was indeed awarded the bus or £100. His choice is not recorded but the judgement seems to have confirmed that there had been something underhand transpiring.

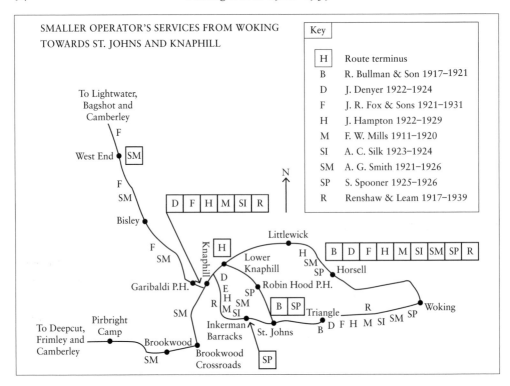

SMALLER OPERATOR'S SERVICES FROM WOKING TOWARDS ST. JOHNS AND KNAPHILL

Key

H	Route terminus
B	R. Bullman & Son 1917–1921
D	J. Denyer 1922–1924
F	J. R. Fox & Sons 1921–1931
H	J. Hampton 1922–1929
M	F. W. Mills 1911–1920
SI	A. C. Silk 1923–1924
SM	A. G. Smith 1921–1926
SP	S. Spooner 1925–1926
R	Renshaw & Leam 1917–1939

In any case, Denyer got the bus one way or another and applied in April 1922 for a licence to run it between Knaphill and Woking; this was granted in July. Denyer continued his fishmonger activities, employing John Fuller to drive the bus. Following an incident outside Highclere Hall in Knaphill on 13 December 1922, Fuller accused Arthur Smith, proprietor of the Blue Omnibus firm, of physical assault after an argument over competitive tactics, having sought a police constable. The case was later heard by Woking Bench. Smith alleged that Fuller had been taking patronage away from his bus by enticing people onto Denyer's vehicle. Smith allegedly took off his coat, seemingly for a fight and Fuller started running away. Smith followed, although witnesses did not see an actual assault nor heard bad language. Smith was fined 10 shillings, presumably for threatening behaviour.

Such incidents no doubt influenced the opinion of the council, who probably despaired of the continuing antics between the various small firms on the St Johns route. Despite uncertainties and vagaries they were tolerated as they provided a useful public service, as people demanded more mobility throughout the 1920s. In the case of Denyer, the council showed its authority in July 1923 when they stated that it would not be in the public interest to renew his licence, perhaps as he had not submitted a timetable. However, the council relented the following month when one was received.

Denyer was present at a meeting with the council in June 1924 to discuss coordination on the Knaphill route, although it appears that he gave up running a bus soon afterwards, thus ending his relatively short-lived public transport activities. By 1915 J. Denyer & Son also had a fish shop at The Broadway, Knaphill and subsequently had premises at 11/13 Percy Street, Woking so perhaps they decided to concentrate on their core business. By 1930 the fried fish shop at St Johns was listed as a partnership of Denyer and Martingell.

Thames Valley

A Major Player Makes a Brief Visit

During the early 1900s the tramway-owning British Electric Traction Co. Ltd (BET) recognised that the motor bus was going to have a bright future as a cost-effective way of feeding people into tram systems from outlying areas and as a way of developing routes in the more rural parts. Thus a number of fledgling territorial bus operations were initiated or bought into, which by 1912 were coordinated by the subsidiary British Automobile Traction Co. Ltd (BAT). Despite the difficulties of wartime conditions it was decided to set up a Reading-based branch of BAT. This started its first services on 31 July 1915, using the fleet name 'British' on single-deck buses in a Saxon green and white livery.

In the following years services were quickly established, radiating out from Reading. By 1920 there was a fleet of thirty-four Thornycroft J-type vehicles. BAT decided that these operations should be consolidated in a new separate company. Thus Thames Valley Traction Co. Ltd came into being on 10 July 1920, owned eighty-six per cent by BET and fourteen per cent by Tillings. The latter was also a large bus-owning conglomerate, which decided to work in partnership with BET to develop networks, rather than compete with them.

Thames Valley had a small garage, in a large barn at Englemere Farm in Blythewood Lane about one mile west of Ascot in Berkshire. Still keen to expand their territory, they considered the rural area southwards towards Woking, where links would be available to A & D services. They already ran to Sunninghill and Sunningdale from Ascot, and in January 1922 announced their intention to extend this service through to Windlesham, Lightwater, Chobham, Horsell and Woking. This was portrayed as being a great boon to residents in the Chobham district as well as allowing Woking people to reach Bracknell and Windsor by changing bus at Ascot.

Woking Council optimistically issued the requested licences to Thames Valley for thirty-two buses and six charabancs, but when Thames Valley's new Ascot to Woking service 3 commenced on 1 May 1922, the regular bus was a Thornycroft J-type, registered DX 2173, fleet number 42. This had a twenty-nine-seat front entrance body by Hora, and had recently been obtained with two others from the Eastern Counties Road Car Co. that had inherited them from the Great Eastern Railway.

By September 1922 Thames Valley were advising Woking Council that the Chobham to Woking section of the route not surprisingly carried the heaviest traffic. By reducing

Paul Lacey suggests that a Thames Valley Thornycroft J numbered 42 (DX 2173) was allocated to Ascot depot for the Woking service. It was acquired in April 1922 from the Eastern Counties Road Car Co., just prior to when Thames Valley started their short-lived service 3 extension southwards. The only photograph discovered is of sister vehicle 40 (DX 2174), seen at Bucklebury in Berkshire. Due to a roof defect affecting both No 40 and 42, the centre portion has been replaced with canvas, tied down at the side. (*Paul Lacey Collection*)

the Ascot to Chobham section to merely garage 'positioning' journeys at the start and end of the day, they could provide more trips from Chobham to Woking with one bus, catering for demand. This change does not seem to have been effected until March 1923 but in the event, Thames Valley decided to abandon the whole of service 3 south of Sunningdale from 1 May 1923, thus ending their brief foray into Woking. They no doubt identified other potential routes on which to deploy the vehicles, with less unremunerative mileage involved. Thames Valley was also facing new competition in the Ascot area, so the company probably was keen to concentrate its resources to combat them. Additionally, other more local operators were turning their attention to serving Chobham and Horsell, and a view has been expressed that Woking Council may not have wholly welcomed the presence of Thames Valley, being seen as an interloper from Berkshire.

As a postscript it can be mentioned that it was not to be until 5 April 1954 that Thames Valley vehicles reappeared in the Woking Council area on a bus service, and then only on the western extremity. Jointly with A & D they started service 75 from Reading to Guildford via Bagshot, Lightwater, West End, Bisley and Brookwood Crossroads. Eventually, Thames Valley and A &D, under National Bus Co. auspices, were merged on 1 January 1972 to form the Thames Valley & Aldershot Omnibus Co. Ltd – Alder Valley – but that is definitely another story.

J. F. Hampton

An Unremarkable Bus Operator

Yet another operator on the Woking–St Johns–Knaphill route was John Frederick Hampton of St Johns Road, apparently giving Woking Council relatively little trouble, despite the usual occasional competitive irregularities. Unlike some of the other local firms he did not make repeated applications for new services, except in one case where he had temporarily expanded his activities at the request of another operator.

Hampton, like several other bus proprietors, owned a butcher's shop as early as 1911. Seemingly keen to diversify his business activities, he commenced running on the St Johns route in May 1922 when he purchased Arthur Stilwell's twelve-seat Napier vehicle. This was supplemented about two months later with a new fourteen-seat Ford Model T that was a left-hand-drive model. The Napier was replaced in February 1924 by another fourteen-seat Ford. In June of that year, Hampton was noted as running fifteen round trips between Woking and Knaphill, starting at 8.20 a.m. and ending at 1025 p.m. He purchased a Caledon open charabanc around June 1925, but Woking Council refused to licence it although it was kept and used. However on 17 August 1925, his two Ford buses were noted heading off towards Mayford, possibly on a private party outing, thus it could be assumed that his Knaphill bus service was not operating that day.

From October 1926 Hampton was covering the Woking–Horsell–Lower Knaphill service of Stephen Spooner, after the latter's bus had been destroyed by fire. Although he showed some interest in developing the route for himself, he was thwarted by an agreement between Spooner and A & D for the latter to acquire the rights of the service. Although A & D officially acquired the service on 15 December, it is recorded that they actually started operating it three days later, while Hampton's bus was last seen running on 22 December. Possibly to assist with this temporary commitment, but officially as a spare, Hampton had acquired in November another fourteen-seat Ford Model T from J. R. Fox.

A complaint was received by the council in spring 1927 that one of Hampton's drivers had allowed a passenger to sit on his right hand side while driving, which was considered a dangerous practice. This related to the left-hand-drive Ford and until he could have it converted to right-hand-drive, Hampton instructed his drivers not to carry passengers on the front seat. The rest of 1927 and the following year appeared uneventful.

Seeking to consolidate further, A & D agreed in February 1929 to acquire Hampton's business, subject to transfer of the licences for the three Ford buses, the Caledon

From what can be seen of the registration number, this Ford T appears to be PC 8947, owned by John Hampton from July 1922. It stands outside Mills' Garage in Hermitage Road after the latter stopped running buses, so it may have been there for work of some sort to be done, may have been kept there or was perhaps just parked for the photograph. The identity of the four men is not known – can anybody out there help? (*Iain Wakeford Collection*)

charabanc and the right to operate his journeys, which would be integrated with their own services between Woking and Knaphill from 25 March 1929. Woking Council acceded to this but warned A & D that the charabanc had never been licensed by them! This was of little consequence, as A & D seem not to have operated any of Hampton's vehicles and they were soon sold. Having disposed of the buses, Hampton continued to run his butcher's shop.

C. Ross & Son

The Catalyst for Battles on the Chertsey Road

In September 1923 Clifford Levi Ross of 5 Bakers Cottages in Lavender Road, Maybury, applied to Woking Council to introduce bus services from Woking station to Maybury Inn via Maybury Road and to Chertsey via Maybury Road, Bleak House and Ottershaw. These were operated by two fourteen-seat Ford Model T vehicles. Not surprisingly, these routes were advertised as the Maybury, Ottershaw and Chertsey Bus Service and in mid-1924 it was recorded by Woking Council that no complaints about them had been received, which was relatively unusual in terms of the local operators. However, there was some conflict between the timings of Ross and Settle regarding Woking to Chertsey journeys, albeit by two different routes although the timings were adjusted to satisfy both parties. By 1925 Ross also owned Orchard Garage in College Road at its junction with Maybury Hill.

In October 1925 Ross applied to operate between Woking and Ottershaw via Woodham, New Haw and Addlestone. W. Eggleton applied concurrently for a similar route as far as Addlestone, but running via Chertsey Road instead of Maybury Road. In the following month, Ross stated that he would withdraw his application if Eggleton was granted a licence and also asked to use a new twenty-seat Republic vehicle to replace Ford PD 7273 on the Chertsey route, although the latter bus continued to be used on the Maybury Inn service. Neither operator was given permission for their new routes to Woodham and Addlestone/Ottershaw but subsequently Eggleton was granted a temporary licence, although the service did not immediately commence. By April 1926 Ross had withdrawn the Saturday service on the Maybury Inn route before 5.45 p.m.

One of Ross's vehicles was involved in an unfortunate accident in Brox Road, Ottershaw on 19 February 1927. A Mrs Hockley alighted from the bus and was then promptly run over by it. First Aid was administered but unfortunately a doctor had to amputate her leg there in the road, according to the local press. Whether anaesthetic was involved was not mentioned! She was taken to Ottershaw Hospital and apparently afterwards was very stoic about what happened.

In January 1927 Woking & District applied to also link Woking with Chertsey via Woodham, New Haw and Addlestone. This was refused as Eggleton was finally about to start his similar service, which probably commenced on 7 March. Ross took Ford PD 7273 off the road in April 1927 when a new fourteen-seat Morris was delivered. The Ford was re-licensed in June as a spare or relief bus. In December 1927 Ross applied for a half-hourly Sunday evening service on the Woking to Maybury Inn route but this was refused. At that time A & D announced their intention to apply for services from Woking to Ottershaw, Chertsey and Weybridge. This may have been a measure designed to frustrate the ambitions of Woking & District. As Ross was running hourly to Chertsey and half-hourly to Maybury Inn, the potential consequences for him were clear if A & D's applications were successful. In the meantime, Fox was making repeated applications for routes eastward from Woking.

Ross was probably encouraged to accept an offer of £235 from A & D for his four vehicles and his routes, which they acquired from 13 January 1928, thus gaining their first services on that side of Woking. The Maybury Inn service was numbered 47 and they achieved their hourly Woking to Chertsey service by acquisition rather than competition, numbering Ross's erstwhile route as 48. The significant competitive battle on the direct Chertsey route between A & D and Woking & District has already been mentioned.

In autumn 1928, when Ross' wife Julie applied for a maintenance order against him in the courts on grounds of desertion, it was recorded that their son Eric Ross was employed at the Orchard Garage, but the business was stated as being no longer profitable. Not long after that, the garage was sold to G. K. Gibbs.

THE

HOOK HEATH

GARAGE

BUS SERVICE

SINGLE FARES

WOKING STATION
2 York Road
3 2 Star Hill
4 3 1 Allen House
5 3 2 1 Holly Bank X. Roads
6 4 3 2 2 FISHER'S HILL

RETURN FARES

WOKING STATION
— York Road
5 — Star Hill
6 5 — Allen House
8 5 — Holly Bank X. Roads
9 6 5 FISHER'S HILL

Children over 3 years and up to 14 years,
one half Adult Single Fare.

THE

HOOK HEATH

GARAGE

BUS SERVICE

Official

TIME TABLE AND FARES

NOVEMBER, 1935
[until further notice

WOKING STATION & FISHER'S HILL

VIA STAR HILL

Proprietors : W. BULMAN & SON,
HOOK HEATH GARAGE, WOKING
[Telephone 454

14 and 20 SEATER SALOON
COACHES FOR PRIVATE HIRE

Index Publishers (Dunstable) Ltd., Dunstable, Beds.

W. J. Bulman & Son

Much Ado About a Most Insignificant Bus Service

By 1911, Walter James Bulman, born at Oakhill in Somerset in 1865, was a hackney cab driver, being described as a Fly Proprietor of Wych Hill. With his son Walter William Bulman he went on to operate motor taxi cabs from premises at Albion Mews, Chertsey Road/High Street, Woking. He lived at 2 Pineview, Hook Heath, in a road subsequently known as Star Hill. There, he developed Hook Heath Garage; this business survived a fire on 24 June 1917, although it was to be temporarily prevented from trading for a considerable time.

That morning, Walter Bulman was somewhat surprised to see smoke outside his bedroom window, reflected in his shaving mirror! His garage, which was a comparatively new building, had its roof ablaze, due to what was subsequently attributed to a short circuit in the wiring system for the electric lighting. Having called the fire brigade, it took them twenty minutes to come one and a half miles, by which time seven cars, the body of another, a pony cart, a bath chair and various tools were beyond redemption. The damage was estimated at £2,000 although most was covered by insurance.

Hook Heath is a fairly select residential district to the south-west of Woking with many large houses. In the 1920s the house-owners employed numerous servants, some of whom lived in, while others came from the local area. These were to be important sources of patronage for the two bus services that served Hook Heath. Bulman was not the first operator to establish a service – that was Renshaw & Leam in December 1921, as already described. However, the irregularities, rivalry and thwarted ambition of these two operators was to take up much space in the Woking Council Highway Committee minutes and would tediously pre-occupy the council's unfortunate bus inspector, although not in such measure as the affairs of Woking & District and A & D!

Walter Bulman received permission to start a bus service between Woking and Hook Heath (Fishers Hill) via York Road and Star Hill in January 1924. A generally hourly service was scheduled, using a thirteen-seat Chevrolet vehicle. Thus it was that Bulman and Renshaw & Leam were to survive the Road Traffic Act 1930 and share the Hook Heath traffic until May 1939 when the almost inevitable A & D takeover occurred.

As part of a survey of bus services in the district in June 1924, Woking Council identified that as a rule buses of both operators ran to Hook Heath at the same time, whereas one was sufficient for the traffic. It was resolved to seek explanations as to why this was the case and whether changes should be made so as to reduce congestion and give a more useful public service. At times, Renshaw was using two buses and Bulman one in close procession with only half a dozen passengers between them. Both firms agreed to a timetable but if one set of journeys was found more remunerative than the other, they could change their respective rotas monthly. Unfortunately this did not work in practice and soon each firm was complaining about the other, with Renshaw running extra buses. In terms of maintaining the agreement in the interests of the public, Woking Council was impotent although things apparently settled down by November 1924.

Supported by a seventy-eight-signature petition, Bulman applied in January 1925 to extend his service from Fishers Hill to Worplesdon. In preparation for this he purchased a second bus in February 1925. The service to Worplesdon materialised in March 1925, running from Woking (separate to the Hook Heath service) via Mayford, Saunders Lane and Worplesdon Hill to the New Inn, but this does not seem to have been successful, being withdrawn after a few months.

In January 1926, Miss Leam complained that Bulman had allegedly extended his Hook Heath service to the main Bagshot Road. A further complaint came a year later when it was again alleged that the route had been extended beyond Fishers Hill. It transpired that Bulman's driver lived in Saunders Lane and took the bus there during his lunch break. Occasionally a person would board a bus in Saunders Lane on its return to Woking. Although this was of little consequence to Renshaw & Leam, it was an opportunity for them to stir up a little trouble. In April 1927 Bulman tried to extend his route again from Hook Heath to Worplesdon Hill with seven journeys each way.

No photographs of Walter Bulman's first three vehicles have been traced, but PJ 2459, a Bedford WLB with Duple bodywork, arrived in 1932 to effect modernisation of the Hook Heath Garage bus service. Not acquired by Aldershot & District with Bulman's service in May 1939, it is recorded as being in Oxfordshire in 1940 in a non passenger-carrying role. (*J. Higham Collection/ Alan Cross*)

Although permission was refused, Bulman did not wait for the outcome and started anyway on 11 April; after a letter from the surveyor, the extension ceased within a few days. Soon afterwards, Renshaw & Leam tried their 'Saunders Lane lunch/tea break' complaint again, to which Bulman responded that the driver gave a free lift to some people before starting the proper journey to Woking at Fishers Hill. On 28 May the council's inspector observed six people boarding at Saunders Lane after the 'tea break', whereas Renshaw & Leam's bus had only one passenger, for which Bulman received a warning that the practice must not continue. He then applied formally to do this but was refused.

Bulman tried again for an extension to Worplesdon Hill in September 1927, this time accompanied by a petition with forty-one signatures. Renshaw & Leam objected and offered to provide any additional service thought to be necessary, so the application was refused. Notwithstanding this, Bulman tried again no less than five times up to February 1931. However, his ambition for a Worplesdon Hill extension was to remain unfulfilled, despite correspondence with the council when he felt he was being treated unfairly when viewed against the licensed and unlicensed activities of Renshaw & Leam.

The original Chevrolet bus was scrapped after being replaced in March 1928 by a new fourteen-seat Chevrolet. As some compensation for the frustration over the Worplesdon Hill issue, Bulman was allowed in May 1928 to increase the Sunday service between Woking and Fishers Hill from one to five journeys, thus matching the level of service provided on that day by Renshaw & Leam, to the chagrin of the latter. At the end of that year, Bulman was allowed to start three additional journeys on weekdays from Woking to Star Hill and one on Sundays, together with an extra Sunday journey to Fishers Hill.

After bus service licensing was transferred from Woking Council to the traffic commissioner on 1 April 1931, Bulman's Bus Service was allowed to continue and matters were subsequently fairly uneventful, although another attempt (in the first licence application in June 1931) to extend the service to Worplesdon Hill was refused.

In January 1932 a new twenty-seat Duple-bodied Bedford WLB was delivered while in June 1934 a second-hand Dodge with Willmott bodywork replaced Chevrolet PH 8373. The final acquisition was a fourteen-seat Chevrolet coach (MV 148) acquired from Fox of Hounslow in April 1935. In November 1935 there were eleven journeys from Woking to Fishers Hill and three as far as Star Hill on weekdays and six to Fishers Hill and one to Star Hill on Sundays. The single fare from Woking to Fishers Hill was 6d, return 9d and the service was then marketed as the Hook Heath Garage Bus Service.

In April 1939 A & D agreed to pay £150 for the goodwill of the service, taking over on 10 May 1939 – the same day that they acquired Renshaw & Leam's activities. The three remaining vehicles were disposed of separately but Bulman's bus driver transferred to A & D. The bus service was combined with one of those taken over from Renshaw & Leam to form new A & D service 63, which ran from Woking to Worplesdon (Fox Corner) via Star Hill and Hook Heath, surviving until 1980, latterly as Alder Valley service 263.

S. Spooner

An Unlucky Man

By the mid-1920s Woking Council's Highways Committee was already emulating its eventual successor – the traffic commissioner – by refusing licence applications from would-be new entrants to the market if it felt that the intended bus routes were already adequately served. They had become weary of dealing with operators constantly complaining about the proposed and actual activities of each other. However, there were still some who thought they would try their luck against incumbents on what were seen as lucrative corridors, especially as some of the earlier proprietors had ceased running on the St Johns route.

One of these was Stephen Spooner of The Chestnuts, St Johns Lye, who had been advertising his talents of 'Blacksmith, Chimney Sweep and Lawn Mower Repair Man'. In November 1924 he applied to license a fourteen-seat bus to run between Woking and Bagshot. This was refused as the council considered it unnecessary. However, they relented and granted the licence on 9 December, to run via Chobham. Another application from Spooner to run from Woking to St Johns and Inkerman Barracks followed a similar path, leading to approval on 30 January 1925. Spooner's original bus was registered PD 3733, followed in February 1925 by the delivery of another registered PE 1000 – a mark that might be highly prized today.

Predictably it was not long before the first complaint from a rival operator was dealt with. W. Eggleton, already established on the Chobham route, suggested that Spooner was running five minutes in front of his 2.50 p.m. departure from Chobham, although that time did not conform to the timetable Eggleton had submitted to the council in July 1924. According to his own timetable Spooner was correctly departing at 2.45 p.m., so Eggleton may have made an unauthorised change. In May 1925 Spooner applied to extend his St Johns journeys to Knaphill, which the council considered superfluous. Two months later he applied again to run to Knaphill and to extend his Chobham service to Windlesham and Sunningdale, instead of Bagshot, which was approved. However, complaints were received about the unreliability of the Sunningdale service, while on 3 August there was no service by Spooner at all as both buses were taking private parties to Southsea for a day at the seaside. In October the council proposed that only one bus licence be granted to him.

Spooner took a former driver, Henry Elliot, to court in August 1925 on a charge of embezzling thirty shillings. Apparently it had been left to Elliott to make the arrangements for a private party outing, being organised by a lady from Windlesham, on August Bank Holiday to Portsmouth. She paid Elliot a deposit of £3 against a total cost of £6 13s. Spooner's daughter May, who assisted with the business, gave evidence that Elliot handed over various monies before he left their employ on 19 July but some was later found to be missing. Elliot said he left as he was fed up with the very long hours he worked on long-distance private hire. He was found guilty, put on probation for two years and ordered to pay back the thirty shillings.

In November 1925 Spooner proposed to reorganise his activities again with an application for a circular route to Lower Knaphill, out via Horsell and Littlewick Road and back to town by way of St Johns; this was refused, and meanwhile he had been running bus PE 1000, which was unlicensed, on the Chobham route again. The council still refused to licence it. However, they renewed the licence for PD 3733 to run to Sunningdale, but this service was withdrawn in January 1926 when Spooner turned his attention again to a service from Woking to Horsell and Lower Knaphill, with about twelve round trips. A letter of support from a C. W. Stow seems to have done the trick as the licence was granted, and in April 1926 bus PE 1000 was re-licensed to cope with additional traffic on Saturdays. The following month Spooner asked to extend his service from its terminus at The Royal Oak at Lower Knaphill to The Prince of Wales, St Johns via The Anchor Hotel – a veritable tour of public houses. This was accepted in June, subject to the route being along Robin Hood Road, rather than Hermitage Road, perhaps avoiding duplication with other proprietors' services.

In a repeat of the unfortunate event that befell Arthur Smith, Spooner's garage and his remaining bus – an Overland fourteen-seater – were destroyed by fire on 22 September 1926. The building, measuring forty by twenty-five feet, was made of wood and galvanised iron and was situated between his house and the Basingstoke Canal. The flames from the fire reached thirty feet in height, the roof collapsed and injured a fireman, and another man was knocked into the canal by falling debris. Spooner himself had been a fireman and was able to help with getting the blaze, of mystery origin, under control. As the bus had been off the road for repair, May Spooner was out with a car keeping the bus service running.

As the bus was destroyed, Spooner therefore applied for a licence in respect of a taxi with which to maintain his service. However, more bad fortune was on its way as in October the taxi met with an accident, so he arranged for Hampton to cover the Lower Knaphill service on his behalf. Perhaps sensing an opportunity, A & D offered Spooner £100 to relinquish his licence entirely and had they been in a position to offer him a job as a driver they would have offered £50. Concurrently, Hampton applied to run a more frequent service in his own name but A & D's financial inducement was accepted by Spooner, so they asked the council to grant them a licence instead. It was not felt that any one operator had a proprietary right on a particular route, but as Spooner's bus had been destroyed and he had asked the council to allow A & D to acquire the service, it was agreed that the latter should occur. Thus A & D took over the Lower Knaphill service on 15 December 1926, numbering it as service 41.

The next that was heard of Spooner was more misfortune on 16 May 1928, when a car he was driving collided with a motor cycle and side-car at Brookwood Cross Roads. Described then as a blacksmith and general engineer, he was found guilty of failing to stop, being fined £2 and having his driver's licence suspended for three months. His defence suggested that this would cause great hardship for his livelihood, but he was still in business for at least another twenty years.

S. Tanner

Rural Services North from Woking

By 1905 Thomas Tanner was listed as a butcher in the village of Chobham. By 1911 one of his sons, Stanley Tanner, aged twenty-one, was running a cycle agent business from premises on the corner of High Street and Vicarage Road. The first reference to Stanley's passenger-carrying activities appears in the local press in July 1921 when he advertised an unidentified 14 seat charabanc for hire. A year later he acquired a twenty-four-seat Dennis charabanc. The butcher's shop in Chertsey Road was later run by Arthur Herbert Tanner, Stanley's youngest brother, who originally also helped in the cycle business.

Following the tentative efforts of Thames Valley in 1922/3, the buses between Chobham and Woking were run by Messrs Eggleton and Smith, being later joined by Spooner. By early 1925 Smith had withdrawn in order to concentrate on other routes, and this may have presented Stanley Tanner with an opportunity. He successfully applied to Woking Council in February 1925 to operate on the Chobham–Woking route and initially he used the Dennis charabanc. However, in April he took delivery of a twenty-seat Dennis 50 cwt saloon bus and expanded his service to also run on Sunday mornings. By October 1925 he was running thirteen round trips on the service, which terminated at the Burrow Hill end of Chobham village. The name Tanner's Chobham Bus Service was used.

In January 1926 Spooner withdrew his Woking–Chobham–Sunningdale service, leaving Tanner to run alongside Eggleton. By July 1926, Tanner had extended his service to Valley End, Windlesham, Snows Ride and Sunningdale station, subsequent to which a competing application from Woking & District was refused as being unnecessary. In March 1926 Tanner introduced a new eighteen-seat Dennis 30 cwt bus registered to replace the Dennis charabanc. The latter was re-licensed in October as a spare bus for use in emergencies, followed by the arrival in December of another Dennis 30 cwt bus (PF 5831) with nineteen-seat Strachan & Brown bodywork. A further nineteen-seat Dennis (PF 7274) was licensed the following month, while in April 1927 Tanner gained approval to increase the through journeys beyond Burrow Hill to Sunningdale to four journeys each way. As the timetable did not clash with that of Eggleton, this was to be given a one-month trial, which seems to have been successful.

By September 1926 Tanner had approached A & D to ascertain whether they wished to purchase his business for £7,500. This valuation was considered excessive so a purchase was not pursued. However, the following month they offered only £1,400 which was rejected by Tanner.

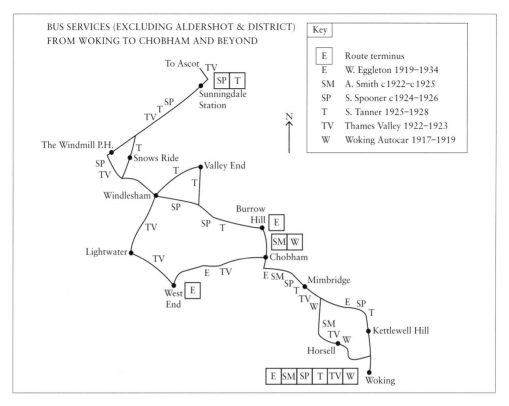

BUS SERVICES (EXCLUDING ALDERSHOT & DISTRICT) FROM WOKING TO CHOBHAM AND BEYOND

Key

E	Route terminus
E	W. Eggleton 1919–1934
SM	A. Smith c 1922–c 1925
SP	S. Spooner c 1924–1926
T	S. Tanner 1925–1928
TV	Thames Valley 1922–1923
W	Woking Autocar 1917–1919

Stanley Tanner's first saloon bus seems to have been PE 2077, delivered in April 1925. It was a Dennis 50 cwt with twenty-seat Strachan & Brown bodywork. Although labelled 'Tanner's Chobham Bus', the trading title of Green Bus Service was also used, giving some indication of Tanner's vehicle livery. (*Mike Stephens Collection*)

Tanner was ready to considerably widen his ambitions in February 1928 when he applied for a lengthy hourly cross-country service from Sunningdale to Guildford via Chobham, Knaphill, Brookwood Cross Roads and Worplesdon. If the adjoining Windlesham and Guildford Councils decided to grant licenses, Woking said they would also do so. A & D responded in protest, saying that if Tanner started the service they would start competing with Tanner on his existing routes. The former two councils gave approval but A & D countered this by announcing their intention to start a Guildford to Windsor service on 23 March 1928, as described earlier. The clerk of Woking's Omnibus Sub-Committee wrote to A & D stating his committee and council would 'be very annoyed if you commence any service in the district without giving them the opportunity of expressing their opinion on the subject'. The tone of A & D's reply was significant and worth quoting from in detail.

> We would point out that this service will operate over twenty-five miles between two important towns and that only three miles are within the Woking Urban District. A very serious position therefore arises if (the start of) such a long distance service is delayed in order that a local authority may be given the opportunity of expressing an opinion on the small portion of the route that lies in their area. In our opinion, the service will be in the interests of the public and has been approved and urged by the Windsor Council. It appears hardly in accordance with public policy that the start of such a service should be delayed until your Council meet in four weeks time. However, we have cancelled its introduction in spite of the fact that timetables have been printed and extra staff engaged.

While Woking Council may have been indignant that their parochial licensing powers had been rebuffed by A & D, the latter's traffic manager must have been enraged that the council was indulging in protectionism and was seemingly supporting the Tanner application. The latter was quite likely as Woking Council had already expressed displeasure at A & D's cavalier attitude to their opinions, and may have been keen to support the more local operator. A & D's reply continued

> We are disappointed that Mr Tanner has been granted this licence as his service will operate over considerable distances covered already by this company and we feel that the understanding reached with the council at the meeting in Summer 1926 has to some extent been broken, so in fairness we trust that the service will now be approved as amended.

The surveyor reported that the road between Castle Grove in Chobham and the Garibaldi P. H. in Knaphill was narrow and of poor construction, with no footways. The council's inspector felt that the hourly service proposed by Tanner was adequate but that if the committee felt that they must allow A & D's application, the two services should be timed so as not to clash with each other. In the meantime, Tanner successfully applied to operate through to Sunningdale from Woking on Sundays with four journeys. In April 1928, Tanner was still intending to start his Guildford service when new buses had arrived from the manufacturers. However, circumstances were soon to alter, as in June A & D offered Tanner £2,000 for his business although negotiations were abandoned temporarily the following month. Discussions were reopened, as a result of which Tanner did not start his Guildford service and A & D did not run to Windsor, although there were other reasons for the latter not occurring. By mid-September, A & D had come to terms with Tanner and asked Woking Council to transfer the licences for three Dennis buses.

On 8 October 1928, by which time Tanner was marketing his operations as The Green Bus Service, A & D took over those three buses and Tanner's services. These were numbered 55 (Woking–Chobham–Burrow Hill) and 55A (Woking–Chobham–Burrow Hill–Valley End–Windlesham–Sunningdale). Tanner retained the High Street garage premises, which became an A & D outstation. Interestingly the takeover did not include Tanner's most recent vehicle, Dennis PF 7274, which must have been sold separately. Dennis charabanc PC 9313 was retained by Tanner with his garage until about September 1931, A & D having departed. Subsequently, Stanley and his wife Grace took over the family owned butchers' shop in Chertsey Road. Following his death, Grace employed another butcher and carried on for several years. In the 1950s it is recalled that Grace would drive the delivery van very slowly around the district, causing large, impatient queues of cars to form behind her.

PE 9850 was an eighteen-seat Dennis 30 cwt., new in March 1926. It was quite similar to many contemporary small Dennis buses in the Aldershot & District fleet, so it probably looked at home when acquired by A&D with the Tanner business in October 1928 and numbered D239. (*R. Marshall Collection/East Pennine Transport Group*)

A. T. Locke & Son

A Guildford Operator Reaches Woking

By 1903 Arthur Tom Locke was in business as a coal and coke merchant. By 1919 he was at 75 Stoke Road, with a coal yard at the Woodbridge Road end of Stocton Road. Having progressed from horse-drawn to motor propulsion, by 1923 Locke was also listed as a removal and haulage contractor.

The first reference to a passenger-carrying vehicle appears in the minutes of the Guildford Watch Committee in January 1925, when a fourteen-seat bus, registered PD 4646, was inspected. This was soon joined by a Ford Model T, registered PD 3871, first licensed in late 1924. This was followed later by PE 1800 of unknown manufacture. These vehicles were used to initiate two bus services, probably very early in 1925: Guildford to Ripley via Burpham and Burnt Common, as well as Guildford to Send (Cartbridge) via Burpham and Wood Hill. The Ripley service supplemented London General 115 (Kingston–Esher–Cobham–Ripley–Guildford), which started on 20 July 1921. In September 1925, PE 6313 was added to the fleet, being a twenty-seat coach on a Ford T extended chassis. Locke used the trading name of Blue Saloon, giving indication of his vehicle livery.

Woking Council received an application in November 1925 from Locke to extend the Send service to Old Woking, which they refused. Then, in December 1925, Locke applied to run a new service from Guildford to Woking via Stoke, Jacobs Well, Sutton Green, Westfield and Kingfield Green. This would run every forty-five minutes using two buses, competing with Messrs Stilwell and Trigg, who were already established on the route. Woking Council would not authorise this, and Guildford Watch Committee delayed giving their response but were encouraged in late February 1926 by Locke to do so, as Trigg was to imminently withdraw his service. No doubt frustrated by the delay, Locke asked Woking Council in April 1926 to reconsider. This time they were prepared to grant licences if the service terminated on the south side of Woking station, rather than in The Broadway on the north (town) side. The service probably commenced in early June 1926, but only every two hours with eight journeys per day, using one bus on a timetable designed not to clash with Stilwell's bus.

After only six months, in March 1926, the body of Ford PE 6313 was transferred onto a new Graham Bros chassis, registered PE 8539. No doubt the Ford chassis had proved unsatisfactory and Guildford's Chief Constable noted that the new one was certainly stronger. By June 1926 a vehicle registered PE 9737 had arrived, followed in September by PF 4135.

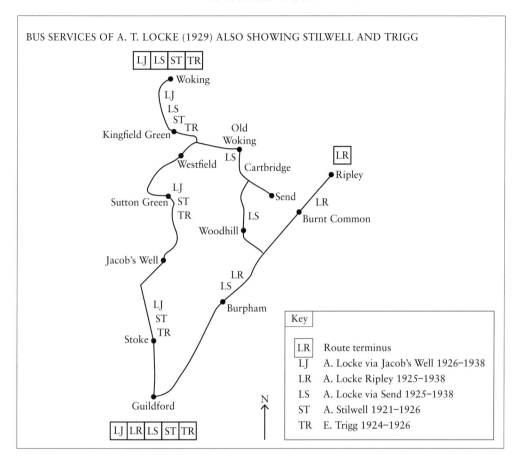

BUS SERVICES OF A. T. LOCKE (1929) ALSO SHOWING STILWELL AND TRIGG

Key

LR	Route terminus
LJ	A. Locke via Jacob's Well 1926–1938
LR	A. Locke Ripley 1925–1938
LS	A. Locke via Send 1925–1938
ST	A. Stilwell 1921–1926
TR	E. Trigg 1924–1926

As Stilwell had now withdrawn his service via Sutton Green too, Locke asked Woking Council in July 1926 to consider allowing him to transfer his terminus to the north side of Woking station, which was then permitted. At that time, the two Locke vehicles licensed for use in Woking were PD 4646 and PE 9737, which were joined by PF 4135. Permission was granted in early December 1926 to double the frequency of the Guildford-Woking service to hourly.

Like many other small bus operators, Locke's drivers sometimes overloaded their vehicles. On 7 May 1927 at 9.40 p.m., Police Constable Thayer stopped Albert Hester, who was driving Blue Saloon vehicle PD 4646 up North Street, Guildford. It was carrying fourteen seated passengers, four standing and four adults sitting on the laps of seated passengers. When PC Thayer opened the door of the bus, a lady sitting close to it said 'shut the door or I shall fall out'. Albert was told he would be reported for overloading but made no response. In defence of his driver, Locke wrote to the Chief Constable, stating that three men had entered the bus through the rear emergency door after it had left the Ward Street terminus. He conveyed his apologies that this was allowed to occur and would do his utmost to prevent it happening again. In spring 1927, two new buses of Guy manufacture entered the Locke fleet – twenty-seat PF 9527, replacing PD 3871, and twenty-six-seat PH 1172. The latter replaced PD 4646 which was scrapped.

Locke allowed twenty-five minutes for his buses to travel the 7.75 miles from

Ford T PD 3871 was one of the first buses owned by Arthur Locke for his Blue Saloon business. The PSV Circle has recorded it as new in November 1924 to J. R. Fox and if this is right, he must have kept it for about a month, which seems somewhat unlikely. The man might be Arthur Locke himself. (*Alan Lambert Collection*)

Carrying fleet number BS4, this Blue Saloon vehicle could be PE 9737 or PF 4135, which have not so far been identified. (*N. Hamshere Collection*)

Guildford to Woking. Apparently, drivers had to exceed the 12 mph speed limit in order to keep to time, and in November 1927 Maurice Sadler was in court for driving at 30 mph. Police Superintendent Boshier thought that Locke's drivers were the worst local offenders for speeding, and Sadler was fined twenty shillings, as was Arthur Locke for 'aiding and abetting'. The latter promised that timetables would be eased forthwith.

Also in November 1927, Locke applied to run the hourly Woking to Guildford service with two buses and to extend the service from Woking station to Mayford. As the decision on whether to grant the latter was deferred, Locke revised his plans to instead use the spare time available to run short journeys from Woking out as far as Sutton Green, giving two buses per hour over that section. This was permitted by Woking Council. In spring 1928 Locke acquired two more buses – PH 8431, which was a twenty-seat Thornycroft with Arnold & Comben bodywork, and PK 1639, of unknown manufacture. In February 1929 came PK 5639, which was a Star Flyer VB4 with twenty-seat Duple body. By this time, Locke's son (Arthur Tom Jr) was involved with the business that was then named A. T. Locke & Son, trading as Blue Saloon Coaches. There was a garage at the Stocton Road premises.

As already described, East Surrey Traction Co. wished to extend their service 31 (Guildford–Send) to Woking via Old Woking and Kingfield Green, and applied to do so in July 1929, at the same time as Locke decided to do the same with his Send service. Blue Saloon buses would work in a circular fashion from Guildford to Woking via Send, returning via Sutton Green, or vice versa, while the Woking to Sutton Green short journeys would be replaced by the new arrangements. As this would not increase the number of buses actually entering or leaving Woking, the application was granted in September, despite objections from Woking & District, unlike East Surrey's, which was refused. In Send, Locke's route double-ran from the New Inn at Cartbridge, down to May's Corner, before turning and heading back to Woking. The new service structure commenced on 21 October 1929, with the Ripley service then running every thirty minutes and the Woking services hourly. All ran daily, although there were fewer journeys on Sundays. On the timetable leaflet, Ripley was shown as numbered 1 and 4, Woking via Send as 2 and 5 and Woking via Sutton Green as 3. Thereafter, the services were little altered for the rest of Blue Saloon's existence, and all successfully gained licences in 1931 under the Road Traffic Act regulations.

From 1930 onwards, additional and replacement vehicles continued to be taken into the Blue Saloon fleet. June 1930 brought a second hand twenty-seat Star Flyer VB4 coach, while a new twenty-four-seat model of the same type was acquired a year later. A locally produced Dennis GL (PL 3022) was purchased in October 1930, before a switch was made to twenty-seat Guy vehicles. These included Victory models in June 1932 and June 1933, and two Wolf models in early 1935. In May 1935 a thirty-two-seat Dennis Lancet coach was purchased (CPH 130) and this became pride of the fleet. It was named Silver Jubilee, to celebrate twenty-five years of the reign of King George V. Three Dennis Ace buses came next – in 1936 and 1937. These had Dennis bodywork, and Dennis also produced the body on the last vehicle to be acquired – EPL 628 – another Dennis Lancet coach, but a rare normal control model that arrived in March 1937. By 1934 Locke had moved his house and office to 16 Stoke Road, and these premises were later renumbered to 38.

Some information on the long working hours and relatively low wages received by the staff of some bus companies was given to Guildford Town Council in April 1931. Blue

From the Red Indian head on the radiator, one might assume this vehicle is of Guy manufacture. It may be PH 1172, recorded as a Guy BB with United twenty-six-seat bodywork. (*E. Nixon Collection*)

PH 8431 was new in April 1928, a twenty-seat Thornycroft with bodywork by Arnold & Comben. (*E. Nixon Collection*)

Although fitted with a Guy radiator, Locke's PK 5639 was a Star Flyer VB4 with Duple twenty-seat bus bodywork, new in February 1929, after Star had been taken over by Guy. After sale from Blue Saloon, PK 5639 passed to West Sussex Fire Service. (*J. Higham Collection/Alan Cross*)

Saloon drivers were working seven and a half- to nine-hour shifts without breaks, with only one driver receiving as much as £3 per week. This resulted in a sixty- to sixty-seven-hour working week. Sunday duties were worked on alternate weeks between 9 a.m. and 11 p.m. – fourteen hours without a break. Conductor Cox had received a letter from A. T. Locke junior advising him of longer working hours without extra pay. When Mr Cox challenged this he was told to accept it or leave, being informed that 'there were plenty of married men with families ready to accept and glad to have it'. After deductions, his wage was £2 6s 2d a week. Perhaps this highlights the somewhat difficult employment conditions in the 1920s and early 1930s when the depressed state of the British economy meant that too many people were chasing too few jobs, giving the employer the advantage. The aforementioned Sunday duties on the Woking services involved a change of drivers in Send. Pat Clack recalled that her mother would provide the crews with tea and cakes in her house, while any passengers were obliged to wait patiently outside in the bus. As with most rural bus services, some regular passengers are remembered for years afterwards. One lady from Sutton Green was known by Locke's crews as 'Woking News & Mail' – the local newspaper. She knew everything about everybody's business and was a great source of local gossip.

Following its formation on 1 July 1933, the London Passenger Transport Board was keen to acquire all other operators of bus services within its designated area. As early as October 1933, London Transport and A & D agreed to work together to acquire the Blue Saloon business if an opportunity arose, as Locke's bus routes fell both within and without the board's area. Negotiations must have been somewhat protracted as the acquisition event did not occur until more than four years later.

On a copy of Locke's timetable that is held by the Omnibus Society's Library, there is a mysterious hand-written note that for the whole month of December 1937, the Blue Saloon services were not operated (managed?) by Locke but by London Transport and A & D, as a 'reprimand for running an unlicensed school service'. Whether the 'reprimand' had been a traffic commissioner's decision is unclear. In any case, on 12 January 1938 the business was formally acquired by A & D, who retained the Guildford–Sutton Green–Woking service, numbering it 29, the excursions and tours licence, and three vehicles. These were Star Flyer PL 8827, Dennis Lancet CPH 130 and Dennis Ace DPD 858. The Guildford to Ripley and Guildford–Send–Woking services were immediately sold to London Transport, who numbered them 415 and 438 respectively. LT also acquired eight vehicles, none of which were operated by them. These were Star Flyer MT 1973, Guy Victory PJ 5970 and APG 207, Guy Wolf CPA 875 and CPE 222, Dennis Ace DPD 859 and EPK 29 and Dennis Lancet EPL 628. The Blue Saloon business was sold for £10,000 and seventeen drivers and conductors transferred to London Transport or A & D. After the passing of routes and vehicles to LT, A & D were left with a net expense of £2,661, including £1,371 for the goodwill of the Guildford–Sutton Green–Woking service.

Although Locke's bus and coach activities were at an end, the Blue Saloon name did not disappear completely. It is really outside the scope of this book, but it is probably worth recording that one of Locke's drivers, John Lambley from Onslow Village, having transferred to London Transport in 1938, started a taxi and hire car business in 1945 that eventually became ABC Taxis (J. Lambley) Ltd. By 1963 he had purchased Locke's house and office at 38 Stoke Road. From 1960 a small fleet of coaches was also operated under the revived Blue Saloon name, and local bus services around Guildford, to Boxgrove Park

Another Blue Saloon vehicle not identified is PK 1639. This might be it and there is strong evidence in the photograph that it was bodied by E. D. Abbott Ltd of Farnham. (*E. Nixon Collection*)

Dennis GL PL3022 is seen looking extremely smart when new in 1930. By April 1936, it had passed to Gilbert and Herbert Gunn's Safeway business in South Petherton, Somerset. (*Alan Cross Collection*)

APG 207 was a Guy Victory with twenty-seat bodywork by United, new in June 1933. Seen in Guildford, adjacent to it is one of A&D's small Dennis buses on service 27 to Guildford Park. (*Andrew Porter Collection*)

and Charlotteville, were started in 1973. An infrequent bus service was started in August 1981 from Guildford to Woking via Send Detention Centre, Ockham, Ripley and Pyrford. This was the first bus service into Woking run by an 'independent' operator since 1939, as opposed to London Transport and A & D, or their successors London Country Bus Services or Alder Valley respectively. The firm was eventually run by Malcolm Lambley, one of John Lambley's sons, and continued until March 1996, when it ceased trading. Its operations and six of its coaches were then acquired by the London & Country Group.

During 1936/7, Blue Saloon obtained three locally-built Dennis Ace vehicles. These twenty-seat buses were known as 'flying pigs', due to the snout-like appearance of the bonnet. Two of these passed to London Transport, but DPD 858 was retained by Aldershot & District, being withdrawn in 1943. (*R. Marshall Collection/East Pennine Transport Group*)

When Dennis Lancet CPH 130 was delivered in May 1935, it was labelled as 'Blue Saloon Silver Jubilee Coach', commemorating 25 years of the reign of King George V. It stands alongside Stoke Park on the Guildford Bypass. (*Malcolm Lambley Collection*)

H. T. Lintott

Buses Were a Family Affair…

As late as 1927, in order to reach Guildford by bus, from Lightwater, West End and Bisley one had to take A & D's service 34, which took a circuitous route via Woking. From Knaphill and Brookwood, it was necessary to use A & D service 28, which ran via Pirbright. The proposals of Renshaw & Leam and Stanley Tanner for services from the western extremity of the Woking Urban District to Guildford have already been mentioned, together with the aggressive but unfulfilled response from A & D, who were trying to prevent the smaller firms from expanding their territory. Concurrent to the foregoing, another omnibus proprietor made a successful bid to provide a service to Guildford and for good measure to extend northwards through sparsely populated countryside to reach the Berkshire town of Bracknell. This was Henry Thomas Lintott of Woodville, Guildford Road, Lightwater.

Various members of the Lintott family had bus-operating interests, and in late 1930 for a short time these were in four locations in the Home Counties. First off the mark was Harry Lintott, who was based in St Albans, Hertfordshire. He was joined by his brother Frederic James in January 1928. Harry was a war veteran, like many of his contemporaries; he undertook a course in engineering at Loughborough Technical College and then went to work mainly as a mechanic for Sydney Hayter's and Frank Hutchins' Yellow Bus Service in Guildford. After surgery on his war-damaged leg he worked as a chauffeur, finally arriving in St Albans in June 1927 with a sixteen-seat Chevrolet purchased from Yellow Bus. He went on to develop several routes in that area as District Omnibus Services, with buses in a distinctive green livery. He purchased some fifteen vehicles up to the time when he sold the remains of his business to Charles Russett & Son in December 1930, as a result of some financial difficulties.

Meanwhile, Harry's and Frederic's father Henry (Harry Sr) owned the Lightwater Motor Garage. In December 1927 he approached Windlesham Urban District Council for permission to run a daily service from Bracknell to Guildford via Bagshot, Lightwater, West End, Bisley, Brookwood Crossroads, Fox Corner, Worplesdon and Stoughton. This was of concern, as although the application had merit, it had the potential to upset an arrangement brokered earlier by Woking Council between various operators including A & D and Fox. There was also the question of the Renshaw & Leam application for a Guildford service, then being considered. Windlesham Council felt it best to grant Lintott's application rather than Renshaw & Leam's as Lintott was not a party to the Woking understanding and as there was some doubt that Renshaw & Leam were ready to start their service as all their buses were already in use on other services. On 2 February 1928 Windlesham Council acceded to Lintott, apparently in order to help Woking Council avoid disturbing the agreement, and as no objections had been received from other operators, assuming they knew of the application. Shortly afterwards Guildford Town Council did the same. It may have been these multi-council considerations which contributed to thoughts of setting up of the Motor Omnibus Through Services Conference on 30 October 1928.

Lintott's service commenced in April 1928 under the apt title of Direct Bus Service. Operations were launched with a fourteen-seat Chevrolet with Thurgood bodywork, which had been transferred from St Albans. Although running for a relatively short distance through Woking Council's area, he had not been licensed by them to pick up passengers between Beaufort House and Fox Corner. In May 1928 he applied for permission to do so and to divert the service via Knaphill (Garibaldi P. H.) and Chobham Road, rather than direct via Bagshot Road. A & D, Fox, Tanner and Renshaw & Leam belatedly voiced their displeasure, suggesting that an extra service was not necessary. The following month it was decided that a Woking licence would be granted, although not for the Knaphill diversion. Subsequently the diversion did start but Lintott gave an undertaking not to pick up passengers in Chobham Road. In November 1928 the number of journeys was increased from six to nine and a second Chevrolet vehicle registered was introduced. A third Chevrolet arrived in May 1929.

Before the cessation of Harry's operations in St Albans, Frederic Lintott took RO 8122, a twenty-seat Graham Bros vehicle with Strachan & Brown bodywork, to operate a service between Basingstoke and Reading via Riseley in July 1930. He had established a motor engineering business and Chevrolet agency in Wote Street, Basingstoke and subsequently started an Odiham–Riseley–Reading service. He used the same title as his father – Direct Bus Service. This venture was short-lived, as he sold the goodwill of his services to Thames Valley on 31 May 1932. Yet another brother, Albert George Lintott, started in October 1930 his Local Omnibus Service, in Petersfield, Hampshire, with Harry Jr as part-owner. Two St Albans vehicles – a Dodge and a Chevrolet – were despatched there to operate a service from Petersfield to Longmoor Camp via Liss, the latter being the Lintott family's home village. When St Albans operations ceased, Harry transferred another three vehicles to Petersfield in December 1930 and a second route linking Petersfield with Liss and Bordon was introduced. However, these ceased in February 1932 and the goodwill of them was sold on 22 April that year to A & D and C. E. Cartwright (Liss & District Omnibus Co.), who thus consolidated their own activities over these roads.

This just left Lintott Sr at Lightwater, whose fleet dramatically increased in February 1932 by the arrival of the five buses from Petersfield, being a Dodge, a Guy and three more Chevrolets. His Bracknell–Guildford service was granted a licence in November 1931 under the new Road Traffic Act regulations. There were nine journeys each way between Guildford and Bagshot on weekdays, four of which extended to Bracknell. On Sundays there were six journeys to Bagshot with four extended to Bracknell and also an extra one between Guildford and Knaphill (Garibaldi), all requiring one vehicle in theory. In May 1932 Lintott applied for a circular service from Lightwater

Henry Lintott supplemented his 'Direct' fleet when five vehicles were transferred from one of his sons – Albert – when the latter ceased operating in February 1932. Three of these were Chevrolets, including UR 4044, which was new to H. R. Swatman of St Albans, passing to Harry Lintott in October 1930 and then to Albert two months later. (*J. Higham Collection/Alan Cross*)

Lintott purchased ACG 89, a smart Bedford WLB with Thurgood twenty-seat bodywork, in March 1935. Seen in Guildford, waiting for time before departing to Bagshot, it was purchased by Sidney Ansell and subsequently went to Aldershot & District, but was not used by them. (*J. Higham Collection/Alan Cross*)

After Ansell had purchased the Direct Bus Service, the fleet was then rationalised to four. The only vehicle bought during his period of tenure was EXF 377, an example of the somewhat rare Denis Pike with twenty coach seats. After sale to A&D, it was used by them (numbered D541) until May 1940 and then again from May 1946 until July 1950. (*Alan Lambert Collection*)

via Sunningdale, Sunninghill, Ascot and Bagshot but it was refused three months later, probably as sufficient public need had not been demonstrated. A licence was granted in May 1933 for excursions from Lightwater to Ascot Races and Aldershot Military Tattoo, the latter an extremely popular event at that time, drawing in dozens of buses and coaches on excursions and private hire.

Two new vehicles were purchased – twenty-seat Thurgood-bodied Bedford WLB in 1935, and a twenty-six-seat Dodge RBF with Reall bodywork in 1936, which replaced some of the earlier vehicles. In August 1936, Lintott was in court, charged with allowing a bus to be used with defective brakes. He was fined £1 but was taken ill during the proceedings.

By 1937 Henry Lintott was not well, and with his sons departed elsewhere, his wife Ada lacked day-to-day supervisory help. Investigating the irregularities, having issued a warning in April 1936, the traffic commissioner declined to renew his licences. In January 1937 a hearing was called in the traffic court when it was revealed that A & D were assisting Lintott with the compilation of timetables and fare tables. They also offered to allow one of their inspectors to supervise Lintott's crews, whose on-the-road activities were said to be reminiscent of the chaotic days of the Woking bus wars in the 1920s. Lintott's drivers were allegedly running a minute or two in front of A & D between Fox Corner and Guildford, rather than the scheduled ten minutes, and were sometimes undercharging. Perhaps by being helpful, A & D were positioning themselves to get first refusal if the business was sold. The traffic commissioner would not allow the continuation of the licence in Mr Lintott's name after 30 June 1937, but his wife could apply for a licence if she wished, with one of the sons as a supervisor. However, the garage and bus business struggled on until November 1937 when it was sold, not to A & D, but to Sidney Ansell, after which the Lintotts seem to have left Lightwater.

Ansell was a coach proprietor based at in Peckham, London SE5, so his acquisition of the Direct Bus Service was somewhat curious. Having acquired three Chevrolets, a Guy, the Bedford and the 1936 Dodge from Lintott, he soon disposed of two Chevrolets and the Guy and added a new Dennis Pike twenty-seat coach in March 1938, registered in London as EXF 377. Little change was evident on the bus service, nor in terms of business development. Unsurprisingly, Ansell soon disposed of this satellite operation, selling it to A & D on 8 June 1938, who paid £1,650 for four vehicles and £250 for the goodwill of the operations. Chevrolet UR 5780 and Bedford ACG 89 were immediately sold by A & D, while the Dodge and the Dennis were kept for a few years. A & D obtained a licence for the Guildford–Bagshot part of the bus service, numbering it 62, but it only had a short life. A direct Bagshot–Guildford service (that is, not via Woking) was not provided again until 1954.

Aldershot & District 1931-39

The 'Tracco' Becomes Respectable

We rejoin the Aldershot & District Woking story just before the implementation of the Road Traffic Act 1930. Although the new Act involved statutory obligations for bus companies in terms of vehicle maintenance and bus, driver and conductor licensing, an organisation like A & D was well placed to fulfil the new requirements. While the need for road service licences would have to be proved in the traffic courts, with potential for objections from other operators, A & D had either acquired most of the significant competitors in the Woking area, or was about to. A & D's operating area had more or less developed to its maximum extent and there was less opportunity for ground-breaking expansion.

Of most relief to A & D was the fact that they would no longer have to deal with a plethora of local authorities in order to gain or renew their licences, with all the parochial vagaries that entailed. Their network development would henceforth see an entire proposed new or amended service granted or refused as a single entity, rather than suffer a setback due to the views of a local council which had jurisdiction over a small part of it. A major commercial advantage was that A & D and others would be spared the effect of damaging competition as the new traffic commissioners would be exercising quantity control as well as regulating fares. This meant that in future, different operators running over common sections of route would be expected to 'come into line' with each other in terms of what they charged to travel. In the 1928/9 financial year, A & D had made a loss of some £5,100 with no dividend being paid to the shareholders. This was due to additional expenditure to counter intense competition, such as around Woking, involving the use of extra vehicles as 'chasers', running supplementary services and maintaining uneconomically low fares.

The acquisition of Woking & District reached fruition on 13 January 1931, involving an agreement between A & D, London General and East Surrey Traction Co. Thus, although A & D was the buyer, London General was to provide the funds to acquire the bus garage, workshop equipment and Fox's house. After deducting those costs, the vehicles and the goodwill of the services were to be funded in the ratio of 74.4 per cent by London General and 25.6 per cent by A & D. Most of the assets and bus services passed to East Surrey via General. However, by nature of its geographical position, A & D retained the service to Knaphill and Camberley (as 34C), which paralleled its own 34/34A, except between the Jolly Farmer and Camberley, where it ran via London Road. The company

ALDERSHOT AND DISTRICT BUS
SERVICES FROM WOKING 1920–1939

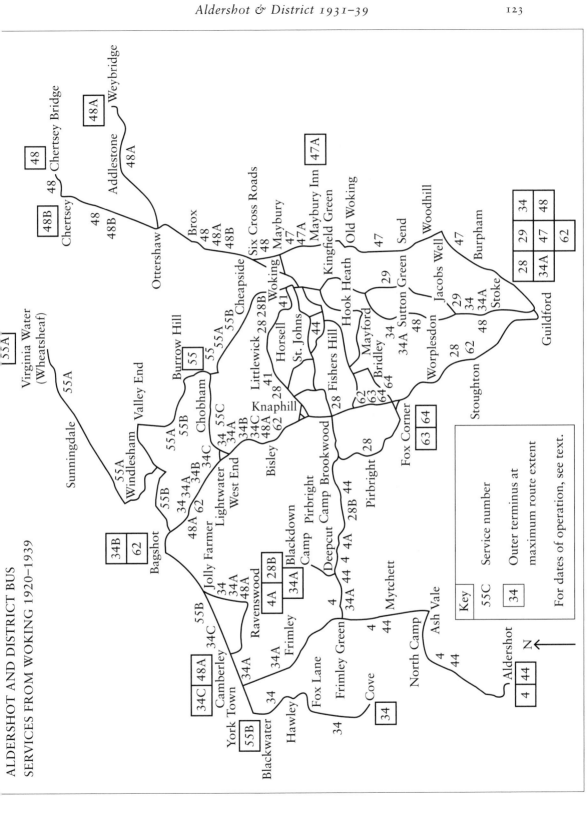

Key:

55C   Service number

34   Outer terminus at
        maximum route extent

For dates of operation, see text.

N
Aldershot

also received the right to acquire the goodwill on a subsequent occasion of the Woking to Chertsey via Ottershaw, part of Fox's service to Windsor. Its share of Fox's vehicles was five Tilling Stevens B10A2 vehicles, registered VB 1272, 4060 and PG 9382/3/4. From 1 April 1931 service 34C was extended from Camberley to Yorktown.

On 1 June 1931 the new bus garage in Goldsworth Road, Woking came into use, allowing East Surrey to take over the lease on the Walton Road premises. An enquiry office at the front of the new garage premises was built for £258 and opened on 1 April 1932. A small building on the forecourt, originally occupied by a tenant running a florist's shop, was taken over by A & D in 1934 for use as an inspector's office.

When applications were made for road service licences, A & D were successful in retaining all their services in the Woking area.

After East Surrey purchased the Bus de Ville business, A & D was to ask East Surrey to immediately withdraw from the Woking to Maybury Inn section. However, plans were already being formulated for the formation of the new statutory London Passenger Transport Board. In summer 1931 it was agreed that A & D would hand over the Maybury Inn route when the board took over, but that they would be allowed to keep their services from Woking to Ottershaw, Chertsey and Weybridge. Matters progressed somewhat faster as Maybury service 47 was transferred to London General Country Services (LGCS) on 1 February 1932 as explained earlier, but there was a dispute over the proposed valuation for the purchase price of £2,644. A sum of £450 was approved as payment to LGCS from 9 February for the goodwill of the Woking–Chertsey route that the latter had been running as part of its service 38. Discussions on the valuation dragged on, but in December 1932 LGCS paid £1,000 to A & D on account for acquiring service 47, and a nominal £1 was added for PH 1106, the Dennis vehicle which was transferred to LGCS as part of the deal.

From 31 March 1932 service 34C was withdrawn and replaced by hourly service 48A (Weybridge–Woking), which was extended to Camberley over the route of services 34/34A, forming an overall thirty-minute headway between Woking and Camberley.

In 1931 A & D took delivery of twelve Tilling Stevens B10A2s with thirty-seat Strachans bodywork, and in 1932 came the first of a very large number of Dennis Lancet single-deckers with Strachans thirty-two-seat rear entrance bodies. The Dennis Lancet was to become the company's standard single-decker for bus and coach work until 1953. For lightly trafficked services, especially in rural areas, A & D purchased firstly twenty-seat Morris Directors of normal control design, which were not successful, and then the Dennis Ace of a similar layout and capacity. The Ace had a protruding bonnet shape somewhat reminiscent of a pig's snout, thus they gained the nickname of 'Flying Pig'. In 1939 came the first nine of the new twenty-seat Dennis Falcon model, again with Strachans bodywork. The concerns of Woking Council and low railway bridges such as the Victoria Arch prevented A & D from using double-deck vehicles in the Woking area between the two wars, thus the Dennis Lancet was the mainstay of the local services. It would not be until 1945 that double-deck A & D buses would first operate from Woking, on service 34B.

W. H. Ross applied to the traffic commissioner for a service from Woking to Horsell via Bullbeggars Lane, through A & D territory. Following objections from A & D and from Woking Council (regarding concerns over the use of certain roads), the application was refused in November 1932. In April 1933 Mr T. Moore of 5 Wilfred Street, Woking

Typifying the Aldershot & District fleet in the early 1930s was OU 7949 (bonnet number TS13), new in 1931, a Tilling Stevens B10A2 with Strachans bodywork. Seen at work on service 48A from Weybridge to Camberley via Woking, it was withdrawn in December 1939 and then saw war service with the Royal Army Service Corps. (*Mike Stephens Collection*)

A&D's new Woking garage in Goldsworth Road was opened in June 1931. This view dates from the early 1960s and shows the enquiry office built in 1961. Among the cars, only the Mini would probably be instantly recognisable on today's roads. Closed by Alder Valley in January 1982, the site was subsequently sold for re-development. (*Peter Holmes Collection*)

applied for a daily service every two hours from Woking to Chertsey, taking a circuitous route quoted in the application as being via Chobham Common, Longcross and Lyne. This was refused and nothing more was heard of Mr Moore. Longcross was not linked to Chertsey until 9 May 1949, when A & D introduced service 48B.

From 21 June 1933 service 55A was extended from Sunningdale Station, via the route of service 1 along the A30, to terminate at The Wheatsheaf public house near the lake at Virginia Water. The A & D route network radiating from Woking was relatively stable through the 1930s but additional services appeared as a result of the takeover of five more independent operators. First of these was the 55C from Woking to Chobham and West End from 9 July 1934, acquired from W. Eggleton Ltd. The twenty-seat Dennis GL, which came with the service, was owned until September 1938.

A & D was the purchaser of the Locke's Blue Saloon business on 12 January 1938. After London Transport had paid for and taken its agreed share, A & D retained the service from Woking to Guildford via Westfield, Sutton Green and Jacobs Well. This gave A & D a third route between the two towns, the others of course being the 28 via Brookwood and Pirbright and the 34/34A/48 via Mayford.

The next acquisition, on 8 June 1938 was of Sidney Ansell's Direct Bus Service from Guildford to Bagshot via Brookwood Crossroads, Knaphill, Bisley, West End and Lightwater. When A & D applied to take over the licence, they did not seek to continue the section northwards from Bagshot to Bracknell, on the premise that there was no public need for it. The service was numbered 62.

However, A & D's decision not to enter Thames Valley territory prompted C. E. & V. M. Jeatt of Winkfield (White Bus Services) to apply for two new services, each with four round trips on weekdays. One was from Windsor to Bagshot, across the Royal Park, which linked to another from Bagshot to Bracknell. At a hearing in October 1938, following an objection from the Southern Railway, the applications were refused on grounds of insufficient evidence of public need. However, the commissioners advised A & D that if need was later demonstrated, that company would be expected to provide something over that road.

A monopoly of bus operations to the west of Woking was achieved on 10 May 1939, when A & D acquired the businesses of the two remaining independents – Renshaw & Leam (Grey Bus Service) and W. Bulman & Son (Hook Heath Garage Bus Service). Renshaw & Leam's journeys between Woking and Knaphill were absorbed into existing service 34B, but the services to the Hook Heath area, Mayford and Fox Corner were somewhat revised. New A & D service 44 was introduced from Woking to Knaphill (Garibaldi) via Star Hill, St Johns and Robin Hood Road; service 63 linked Woking with Fox Corner via Star Hill, Hook Heath, Fishers Hill, Blackhorse Cross Roads and Brookwood Cemetery Gates (incorporating also the Bulman service) and service 64 ran to Fox Corner via Mayford, Saunders Lane, Blackhorse Cross Roads and Bridley. No vehicles were taken over from Bulman but Dennis 30 cwt PG 5551 and Bedford WLBs PJ 239, 8068 and APH 596 were acquired from Renshaw & Leam. A & D decided not to run them and they were sold in a matter of weeks to London dealer H. Lane.

If they did not already know it at the time of the purchases, A & D very soon realised that services 63 and 64 were somewhat unremunerative, even then. At the time of the takeover they amended and reduced the timetables, bringing forth almost immediately a veritable barrage of indignant correspondence from regular passengers from the up-market residential areas of Star Hill, Hook Heath and Mayford. A number of scathing and articulate complaints came from London-bound 'city gents' who used the buses in order to reach Woking Station. Most mourned the disappearance of the Grey Bus and Messrs Bulman. Mr Wallis of Mount Hermon Road wrote, 'I must congratulate you on the new buses – nice curtains, ash trays and sun roof', but the majority of users wanted them to run at a time that would allow them to catch the 7.59 a.m. train. Comtesse Mary de Borchgrave from The Links, Worplesdon Hill, opined that the new timetables were not suitable for her four employees and the many servants employed by others in the area:

> A large number of houses employ servants and nurses; it is hard enough as it is to persuade them to remain when their only means of transport is the very occasional bus which passes and the present charge which is out of all proportion. This is a great blow to householders in this district.

In the face of such criticism, A & D relented and introduced revised timetables with some enhancement as soon as 5 June 1939.

Further service changes before war was declared again were on 24 April 1939, when the Sunningdale Station to Virginia Water (Wheatsheaf) section of service 55A was withdrawn on weekdays and on 2 August when the 64 was diverted between Blackhorse Cross Roads and Fox Corner via Brookwood Cemetery Gates, instead of Bridley.

In summer 1939 Woking Council had aspirations to have a municipally owned bus station in the town at a site in Maybury Road. This was met with some hostility from A & D and London Transport, who would not contribute to the cost of providing or maintaining it. Perhaps they feared that they would no longer be allowed to use their time-honoured stops at places such as The Broadway outside Woking station. Eventually the council decided not to proceed and Woking is without a proper off-street bus station to this day.

The inevitability of another war had been foreseen for some time, especially since Neville Chamberlain had returned from talks with Hitler in Germany, waving a useless piece of paper. The declaration of war came on 3 September 1939 and as in the previous conflict, A & D rose to the challenge, serving as it did Aldershot (Home of the British Army) and numerous other military establishments. Coastal Express services were immediately suspended while vehicle and staff resources were made available for military transport purposes and for transporting evacuees from London from various railway stations in Surrey and Hampshire to reception centres. Some forty-five Dennis Lancet vehicles built in the early 1930s were withdrawn from service for conversion into civilian ambulances to be used in case of major air raids in the larger towns and cities. These events, compounded by the need to economise on the use of petrol and diesel and some general uncertainty about what Germany might do in the short term, gave rise to a programme of service withdrawals or curtailments as an emergency measure.

On various dates in September and October 1939, services 55, 55A (Windlesham–Sunningdale section), 55B, 55C, 62 and 64 were withdrawn, while the 48 was withdrawn between Guildford and Woking between 4 and 17 October and 48A was withdrawn

In 1932, eight Morris Director chassis with Strachans twenty-seat bodywork were purchased, followed by two in 1933 bodied by Abbott of Farnham. This is M9 (CG 3006), one of the latter and quite likely used in Woking. These buses proved most unreliable, so the bodies were re-mounted as early as 1934 onto new Dennis Ace chassis. M9 became D389 (CG 9018). (*Alan Lambert Collection*)

A&D D374 (CG 6400) was an example of the Dennis Ace vehicles purchased in 1934, with Strachans twenty-seat bodywork. When photographed, it was working service 55 Woking to Chobham, acquired from Stanley Tanner. (*Peter Holmes Collection*)

Acquired with the Direct Bus Service of Sidney Ansell in June 1938 was BOR 501 (D1), a Dodge RBF with twenty-six-seat bodywork by Reall, originally delivered to Henry Lintott in September 1936. Sometime between late 1938 and August 1939, it is on Woking working service 55C to Chobham and West End. (*Andrew Porter Collection*)

Representative of the twenty-eight Dennis Lancet buses with thirty-two-seat Dennis bodywork purchased by A&D during 1938 is D523 (COR 176). Seen in Aldershot, it was renumbered 780 in June 1951 and withdrawn just over a year later. (*Mike Stephens*)

Probably seen when new in 1936 is A&D D422 (AOT 602). This Dennis Lancet was one of a pair originally used for military band transport contracts. After wartime use as an ambulance, it was demoted to normal bus work with its petrol engine replaced by a diesel. (*Mike Stephens Collection*)

Arriving just before the war in August 1939, Dennis Lancet/Strachans DHO 295 is representative of the last new full-size single-deckers purchased by A&D during the period covered by this book. Appropriately, it was captured on film in Woking. (*Mike Stephens*)

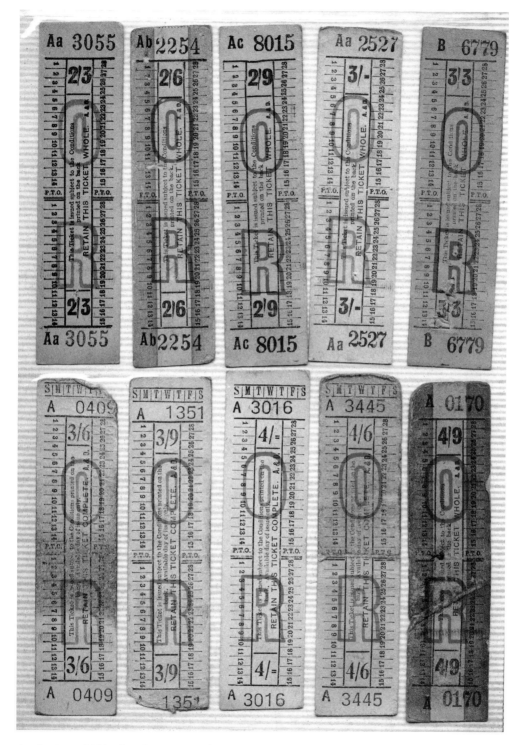

A selection of Aldershot & District tickets. (*Courtesy of Les Smith*)

between Woking and Weybridge from 4 October. The latter was to be reinstated in 1941, but to Chertsey, rather than Weybridge. When the 48 reappeared on 18 October, it was revised to run in two hourly overlapping sections: Guildford to Ottershaw (weekdays) and Woking to Chertsey Bridge (daily).

As the 'phoney war' progressed it was felt possible to reinstate some of the withdrawn services after a few weeks. No doubt there had been public complaints, especially from Chobham. The 55B and 55C were reinstated on 18 October and the 55A was projected back to Sunningdale. On the same date, short service 44 was extended from Knaphill to Aldershot via Brookwood, Pirbright Camp, Deepcut Camp, Blackdown Camp, Frimley Green, Mytchett, Ash Vale and North Camp, to augment service 4, probably to cater for the increasing military patronage. The hourly 44 timetable was revised to operate only in the afternoon and evening. These were therefore the final service changes before 31 December 1939 and the end of the period under review.

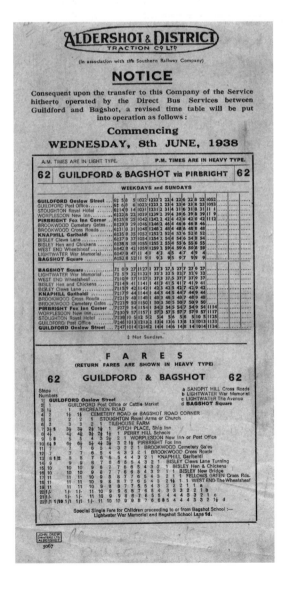

London Transport

Carrying on What General Started

At its formation on 1 July 1933, there was little to show the travelling public that the London Passenger Transport Board had taken over the role of providing the capital's bus services from London General and other operators. The board chose to continue the repainting of country area vehicles into the green and black livery introduced by LGCS in the last months of its existence, but interestingly decided to just show 'General' as a fleet- name, until spring 1934 when the underlined 'London Transport' in gold lettering was introduced. In terms of key leadership figures there was vital continuity – Lord Ashfield was Chairman of the Board, Frank Pick was Vice Chairman and Arthur Hawkins was General Manager of Country Buses and Coaches. As far as Woking was concerned, London Transport's Central Bus Department was running service 79 to Kingston, while the Country Bus & Coach Department ran the 36 and 37 from Guildford or Ripley, through Send, Woking, Addlestone, Chertsey and Egham to Windsor. There was also Green Line service Y from West Byfleet to central London.

The new licensing procedure under the Road Traffic Act was somewhat unkind to Green Line and other coach operators, and there were many appeals to the Minister of Transport over the traffic commissioners' refusal to grant licences and the imposition of restrictions on boarding points and terminal points in London. It was therefore decided to set up a Committee of Inquiry into motor coach services to London, chaired by Lord Amulree. Part of his report recommended that all services should terminate off the public highway, to reduce congestion. In those days of relatively free-flowing traffic on the radial routes, one way of circumventing the terminus issue was to join separate services on both sides of London together to create through services across the central area.

After just three years, the flagship Poland Street Coach Station was closed from 4 October 1933 as it had caused more congestion in the narrow adjacent streets than that it was intended to resolve. As a consequence, from that date Green Line service Y was re-designated BM and extended beyond London to Waltham Cross, Cheshunt, Hoddesdon and Hertford, operation being shared between Addlestone and Ware garages. Green Line previously had a service C from Chertsey to London, which was now paired with a new hourly service AC from Woking to Sevenoaks via West Byfleet, Weybridge, Walton, Kingston, Richmond, Hammersmith, Victoria, Lewisham and Bromley. At weekends, service AC ran beyond Sevenoaks to Tonbridge and Tunbridge Wells. Routes C and AC were jointly worked by Addlestone and Tunbridge Wells garages.

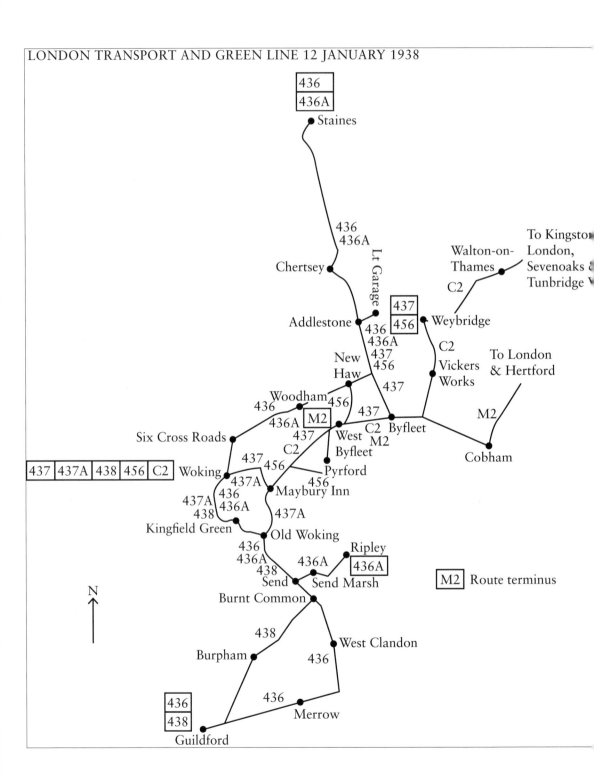

LONDON TRANSPORT AND GREEN LINE 12 JANUARY 1938

In 1933, the premises at Hamm Moor Lane, Weybridge, were enlarged to accommodate buses from the Walton Road, Woking garage, which was closed on 16 May that year. Subsequently, on 24 June 1936 a new purpose-built bus garage was opened in Station Road, Addlestone. Built in the substantial, distinctive and impressive style used by London Transport (LT) for its new garages at that time, it allowed the closure of the Hamm Moor Lane garage.

The last independent operator running into Woking from the eastern side of town succumbed on 2 June 1934 when the firm of W. Eggleton & Son Ltd was acquired by LT. Eggleton's half-hourly service from Woking to Addlestone via Woodham and New Haw was numbered 456, while LT transferred the Chobham route to A & D as already described.

LT had a grand renumbering event on 3 October 1934; service 79 became 219, while services 36 and 37 became 436 and 437. The latter two became routes of epic proportions when they were extended on 3 July 1935 from Windsor to Slough and Uxbridge over the routes of services 458 and 457 respectively. From the same date, the 437 was diverted between Woking and New Haw (Black Prince) via Six Cross Roads and Woodham, while service 456 was diverted between Woking and New Haw (Black Prince) via Maybury, Pyrford and West Byfleet, thus effectively exchanging routes.

A Green Line reorganisation on 8 January 1936 saw service AC re-designated C2 and extended from Sevenoaks to Tunbridge Wells on Mondays to Fridays and service BM renumbered M2. Late in 1936 the T-class coaches on route M2 were replaced by new AEC Q-class coaches with thirty-two-seat Park Royal bodywork (coded 6Q6 by LT). For its time, the AEC Q was fairly revolutionary, with a side-mounted offside under-floor engine and bodywork that has been described as ultra-modern, uncluttered and well balanced. However, compared to previous versions the frontal design was somewhat disappointing.

Yet another revised pattern of service was initiated on 17 March 1936 when the Windsor–Uxbridge sections regained the 457/458 numbers, although for a time buses and crews apparently continued to work through. The hourly 436 (Guildford-Windsor) was diverted between Woking and New Haw (Black Prince) via Six Cross Roads and Woodham and this interworked with an hourly 436A from Ripley that followed the route of the 436 from Send to Windsor. Consequently, the 437 became just Woking to Addlestone, hourly, via Maybury Inn, West Byfleet, Byfleet and New Haw (White Hart), with additional short journeys twice per hour from Woking to Maybury Inn on Saturday evenings. The 456 remained hourly, Woking to Addlestone via Pyrford.

There was a transfer of work between the Central and Country buses on some of the routes south-west from Kingston on 6 October 1937. Service 219, which at times had seen partial operation by LT class six-wheeled AEC Renown single-deckers, was withdrawn between Weybridge and Woking without direct replacement and instead altered to terminate at Weybridge station. The red Central buses were not to return to Woking. The various small vehicles running on services 437 and 456 were replaced by bus versions of the AEC Q-type with more capacity while the 436 and 436A were diverted at Staines Bridge to terminate at Staines (Great Western Railway station), rather than running to Windsor. Some additional capacity on Saturdays was considered necessary for the western end of the erstwhile 219 route, so a new 437A was provided

As a result of the closure of the Poland Street Coach Station in central London, the Byfleet Green Line service was extended across the capital to Hertford in October 1933 and re-designated as BM. This posed view depicts T220 (GN 2015), an AEC Regal with thirty-seat front-entrance body, typifying the early 1930s Green Line Coaches fleet. (*Snook & Son/Pamlin*)

To supplement or replace the Thornycroft vehicles inherited from Woking & District, London Transport transferred to Addlestone garage several others of that manufacturer's A2L type with bodywork by Thurgood, acquired in December 1933 from the People's Motor Services Ltd of Ware. NY6 (UR 7353) works service 437 after truncation in March 1936 to run only between Woking and Addlestone. (*Andrew Porter Collection*)

In summer 1936 the finishing touches are being made to London Transport's impressive new bus garage in Station Road, Addlestone. Judging by the presence of bus crews, it is already in use and has replaced the premises at Hamm Moor Lane, Weybridge. LT bus services in the Woking area were then shared between this garage and that at Leas Road, Guildford. (*London Transport Museum*)

as a Woking circular service via Maybury Inn, Old Woking and Kingfield Green. Initially run with a C-class Leyland Cub from Guildford garage, it subsequently saw a T-class vehicle from Addlestone. The 437 and 456 were principally run from Addlestone and the 436 and 436A were shared between Addlestone and Guildford.

In terms of official vehicle allocations, Woking area services were characterised until 1938 by the mixed bag of vehicles inherited both from General and also from various independent operators taken over – often companies based far away from Surrey. The 436 and 436A were being operated by 1937 with AEC Reliance vehicles of the R class, which were replaced by the AEC Q class from April 1938. Services 437 and 456 which had been the domain of the NY class of Thornycrofts and then various second-hand Leyland Tigers of the TR class and single-deck Leyland Titans of the TD class, then C-class Leyland Cubs and finally Qs, became operated from March 1938 by the AEC Regal T class.

The purchase by A & D of the Blue Saloon business of A. T. Locke required that the latter's services from Guildford to Ripley and Woking via Send were immediately handed over to London Transport. This occurred from 12 January 1938, with the daily service from Woking to Guildford via Kingfield Green, Old Woking, Send, Burnt Common and Burpham being numbered 438. Previously, Locke had run between Send and Burpham via Woodhill but this was amended as that section of route would have taken LT more than the statutory half-mile beyond its limits. LT gained eight of the Blue Saloon vehicles; although they were relatively youthful, the four Guys, three Dennis and one Star vehicle were disposed of two months later as being non-standard. Instead, service

438 was initiated with TR-class Leyland Tigers from Guildford garage, which were replaced after four months with T-class AECs, and then by Qs from January 1939.

In preparation for another war, all Green Line services, including the C2 and M2, were withdrawn after 31 August 1939 so that the coaches could be converted to ambulances to evacuate patients from London hospitals in anticipation of immediate air attack. Subsequently, there was a partial resumption of services and although service C (later numbered 20) to Chertsey was so favoured, Woking was not. This remained the case until post-war reinstatement brought the Green Line back to Woking on 1 May 1946.

Services 437 and 456 were extended from Addlestone to Weybridge and Walton during Saturday afternoons and evenings from early December 1939, as some replacement for route 214 from Kingston via West Molesey, which was cut back to terminate at Walton. For obvious reasons, the output of the Vickers Aircraft Factory at Brooklands near Weybridge was being increased, necessitating a larger workforce including many local women. On 11 December 1939, one source records that a number of new services designed around shift change times at Vickers were introduced. Two from Woking were derivations of services 437 and 456, being numbered 437B and 456B respectively. En-route to Brooklands they served Maybury Inn, West Byfleet and Byfleet (as well as Pyrford on the 456B) and were operated by single-deckers. Additional capacity was needed from Byfleet, so an extra service numbered 459 was provided by a double-decker. Interestingly, these Works Services are not mentioned in the contemporary public timetable booklet, but such discrepancies and uncertainties did occur during those difficult times. However, by March 1940, journeys on services 437 and 456 were extended from Addlestone to Weybridge station on Monday to Friday afternoons and evenings, and these were numbered 437B and 456B. Concurrent with the December 1939 changes, which is journey's end for this narrative, the small LT garage at Weybridge, with an allocation of four buses for services 218, 219 and 219A, was closed on 6 December.

By the mid-1930s, the long services, 436/436A Guildford/Ripley to Windsor, were the domain of the AEC Reliance R class, allocated to Guildford, Addlestone and Windsor garages. R43 (HV 1137) had been purchased by LT in December 1933 with the business of Battens of East Ham and had bodywork by Park Royal. It survived until 1938. (*Alan Cross*)

Another of the former People's Motor Services Thornycrofts, NY5 (UR 7142), works service 456 from Addlestone to Woking on 1 August 1937. (*Les Stitson Collection*)

The T class coaches on Green Line service M2 were replaced in 1936 with new under-floor-engine AEC Q type vehicles. Q228 (DGX 234) represents the Green Line 6Q6 variant. The bodywork by Park Royal was not particularly inspiring in design and the full-width cab contributed to the low seating capacity of thirty-two. (*J. Higham Collection/Alan Cross*)

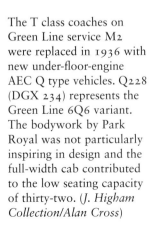

Seen on service 436A heading for Ripley at Woking station is AEC Reliance R41 (HV 62), another former Battens vehicle but with Short Bros. bodywork. Previously used on its former owner's service from London (Aldgate) to Tilbury, it was converted from coach to bus seating. (*G. Robbins Collection/Alan Cross*)

For a few months in 1937/8, the small Thornycrofts based at Addlestone for services such as the 437 and 456 were replaced by larger Leyland buses acquired by London Transport from various operators. Earlier, TD 131 (MV 1019), inherited from Prince Omnibus Co. of Edmonton, was on the 436A, operating from Windsor garage. It was a Leyland Titan TD1 with Duple body. (*Andrew Porter Collection*)

In 1935, thirty-one of the 1929 AEC Reliance chassis of the R class were given new thirty-seat, front-entrance, metal-framed bus bodies by Weymann, but it was only to be three years before the bodies were re-mounted on older AEC Regal chassis of the T class. This is R29 (UU 6603), allocated to Addlestone and working service 436A after the northern terminus became Staines instead of Windsor in October 1937. (*G. Robbins Collection/Alan Cross*)

Another example of the Leyland Titan single-deck buses was TD 185 (GC 7778), previously operated by Premier Line of Slough until December 1933. It had a Duple rear entrance body and, although in Green Line livery, is seen at The Duke's Head in Addlestone, now demolished, en-route to Guildford. (*A. Duke*)

An example of London Transport's acquired Leyland Tiger buses is TR28 (GN 5138), a Leyland TS3 with London Lorries bodywork, seen at Woking station. Like the bus in the previous photograph, it had once been used by Premier Line on their London to Slough/Windsor coach service but was then relegated to local bus services like the 456 when allocated to Addlestone garage. (*Andrew Porter Collection*)

The prototype of LT's somewhat revolutionary TF class (TF 1, DYL 904) had a Leyland FEC chassis and the latter also built the body, with thirty-four seats. Although entering service on Green Line route C2, Woking–Tunbridge Wells, on 1 December 1937, the other eighty-seven members of the class did not arrive until 1939. The flared skirt panels were unique to TF1, as seen in this view at Eccleston Bridge, Victoria, in London. The whole class was withdrawn at the outbreak of war for conversion to ambulances. (*A. D. Packer*)

In this wartime view, Q14 (BXD 535) was working a short journey on the 436 between Guildford and Merrow. Built in 1935, this AEC Q had thirty-five-seat centre-entrance bodywork by Birmingham Railway Carriage & Wagon Co. Ltd and was known as the 4Q4 variant for the Country Bus Department. Similar vehicles were used on services 436, 436A and 438 to Woking at the end of the period covered by this book. (*Les Stitson Collection*)

Bibliography

Books

Akehurst, L., *Green Line* (Capital Transport, 2005).

Barker. T. and Robbins. M, *A History of London Transport Vol. 2* (George Allen & Unwin, 1974).

Blacker. K., Lunn. R. and Westgate R., *London Buses Vol. 2: Country Independents 1919–1939 Part 1* (HJ Publications, 1983).

Brown. S., Dennis, *100 years of Innovation* (Ian Allan, 1995).

Durrant. R., King. J. and Robbins. G., *East Surrey* (HJ Publications, 1974).

Glazier. K., *Battles of the General: London Buses 1918–1929* (Capital Transport, 2003).

Glazier. K., *Last Years of the General: London Buses 1930–1933* (Capital Transport, 1995).

Glazier. K., *London Buses before the War* (Capital Transport, 1995).

Hannay. R., *Dennis Buses in Camera* (Ian Allan, 1980).

Hillier. J. and Sherwin. J., *Glory Days: Aldershot & District* (Ian Allan, 2004).

Holmes. P., *Aldershot's Buses* (Waterfront Publications, 1992).

Lacey. P., *A History of the Thames Valley Traction Co. 1920–1930* (Lacey, 1995).

McCall. A., *Green Line* (New Cavendish Books, 1980).

Townsin.A., *The Best of British Buses:75 years of Aldershot & District* (Transport Publishing Co., 1981).

Wakeford. I. (ed.), *Changing Woking* (Woking Community Play Research Group, 1992).

Wakeford. I., *Woking Town Centre: An Illustrated History* (Wakeford, 2003).

Vehicles Acquired by London Transport 1933–1939 (publication LT6, PSV Circle/ Omnibus Society).

Fleet History of Aldershot & District Traction Co. (publication 2PK3, PSV Circle, 2000).

Magazines & Journals (Selected Issues)

The London Bus Magazine, London Omnibus Traction Society.

Journal of the Aldershot & District Bus Interest Group.

Appendix:
Vehicles of Local Operators

In the interests of space, only vehicle details for the smaller operators are shown. PSV Circle Fleet History 2PK3 (February 2000) gives complete details for the vehicles of Aldershot & District, while there are various books available that list and examine the vehicles of Thames Valley, East Surrey Traction Co., London General Omnibus Co. and subsidiaries, and London Transport. The following tables show all known vehicles, although inevitably much of the detail has not survived. For the period before 1930, most of the information available is that which is recorded in the records of Woking and Guildford Councils, in many cases consisting of just a registration number and the dates licensed. The records are not complete and the first licensing reference might be used as a proxy for the date when a vehicle came into use with that operator, although care must be taken with such assumptions. The Surrey Motor Taxation records of the period are not available, believed destroyed.

A blank in the tables indicates that the particular detail has not been traced.

Notes on Codes Used to Describe Vehicle Bodies

Where possible the standard codes as recognised in most enthusiasts' publications have been used to describe body types and seating capacities.

Prefix:
B: Single-deck bus
C: Single-deck coach (or bus with coach-style seating)
Ch: Charabanc (open or with folding canvas roof), usually with bench seats
O: Open-top double-deck

Figures:
Seating capacity as stated

Suffix:
C: Centre entrance
D: Dual entrance
F: Front or forward entrance
R: Rear entrance (with open platform on double-decks)

R. Bullman & Sons

Woking Council Licence No.	Registration No.	Chassis (& Body where known)	Body Configuration	Former Owner	Date In	Date Out
46	PA 6943	Ford		New	by 5/17	
41	PA 7621	Ford		New	by 6/18	
	BH 2927	Albion	10	Mills, St Johns	5/21	by 1/22

W. Bulman & Son

Woking Council Licence No.	Registration No.	Chassis (& Body where known)	Body Configuration	Former Owner	Date In	Date Out
173	PD 8627	Chevrolet	13	New	1/24	/28
196	PE 1019			New	2/25	1/32
230	PH 8373	Chevrolet	14	New	3/28	8/34
-	PJ 2459	Bedford WLB-Duple	B20F	New	1/32	5/39
-	RX 8375	Dodge-Willmott	B14F	Ranger, Maidenhead	6/34	5/39
-	MV 148	Chevrolet U	C14	Fox, Hounslow	4/35	5/39

P. R. Burton

Woking Council Licence No.	Registration No.	Chassis (& Body where known)	Body Configuration	Former Owner	Date In	Date Out
	PC 5209		20	New	8/21	9/23

J. Denyer

Woking Council Licence No.	Registration No.	Chassis (& Body where known)	Body Configuration	Former Owner	Date In	Date Out
6	CT 351	Brasier	8	Jenner, St Johns	by 4/22	/24
	PB8935	Napier	12	Hampton, St Johns	2/24	/24

W. Eggleton

Woking Council Licence No.	Registration No.	Chassis (& Body where known)	Body Configuration	Former Owner	Date In	Date Out
76	PA 7553	Ford		Woking Autocar	8/19	
158	PC 9660	Ford		New	by 1/23	4/30
162	PD 6394	Ford	Ch14	New	by 5/23	
178	PB 8829	Ford	Ch14		4/24	
192	AK 1478	Renault	12		11/24	by 4/25
198	PE 2505	Republic	20	New	by 4/25	4/28
207	PE 7077	Republic-Coulter	B18	New	7/25	3/31

	Registration No.	Chassis (& Body where known)	Body Configuration	Former Owner	Date In	Date Out
47(A)	PD 3871	Ford T-Coulter	14	Locke, Guildford	2/27	by 12/28
(B)	PE 3884	Ford T	14	Pullen, Guildford(?)	by 4/27	by 12/27
222	PH 1319			New	by 6/27	9/29
227	PH 5276	Dennis 30cwt	B18F	New	10/27	6/34
198	PH 8572	Thornycroft A2	B20F	New	4/28	2/33
240	PG 3194	Dennis 30cwt	B18F	New	9/29	6/34
158	PG 8716	Dennis GL	B18F	New	4/30	6/34
-	PL 5896	Dennis GL	B20F	New	3/31	6/34
-	PJ 7438	Dennis GL–Dennis	B20F	New	7/32	6/34

Note (A): Chertsey Council Licence No.

Note (B): As listed in Woking Council Minutes 3/6/27 but maybe an error.
A vehicle with this registration was owned by F. T. Pullen, Guildford and was recorded as scrapped 2/27 after collision damage, so doubt exists.

J. R. Fox & Sons

Woking Council Licence No.	Registration No.	Chassis (& Body where known)	Body Configuration	Former Owner	Date In	Date Out
139	PB 8110	Ford T-Fox	8	Converted from a car	4/21	4/24
		Ford T			/21	by 9/24
159	PB 8665	Ford T	14	Tanner, Camberley	12/22	5/25
169		Ford T	14		by 11/23	by 9/24
	PD 8852	Ford T-Coulter	14	New	2/24	

175	PD 7993	Ford T-Coulter	14	New	3/24	11/26
139	PD 9596	Ford T-Coulter	14	New	4/24	by 3/29
181	PD 1347	Ford T-Coulter	14	New	5/24	by 6/29
185/224	PD 2599	Ford T-Coulter	14	New	8/24	12/24
	PD 3871(A)	Ford T-Coulter	14	New	11/24	12/24
191	PD 4089	Berliet	20	New	1/25	2/27
193	PE 1294	Berliet	20	New	2/25	9/29
179	PE 1870	Ford T	14	New	2/25	by 6/29
159	PE 2171	Ford T	Ch14	New	4/25	by 9/29
203	PE 6984	Daimler CM36	B26	New	11/25	1/31
175	PE 8157	Ford T	14	New	1/26	by 6/29
217	PE 8642	Daimler CM36	B26	New	2/26	1/31
197	PE 9993	Daimler CK36	B20	New	3/26	1/31
220	PF 7317	Thornycroft A1	B14F	New	2/27	1/31
191	PF 7461	Thornycroft A1	B14F	New	2/27	1/31
226	VB 1272	Tilling Stevens B10A2-Wilton	B32R	New	12/27	1/31
229	OT 7822	Thornycroft LB	B29F	New	3/28	1/31
234	VB 4060	Tilling Stevens B10A2-Wilton	B32R	New	11/28	1/31
235	VB 4550	Thornycroft A2L-Wilton	B20F	New	1/29	1/31
181	PG 998(B)			New	6/29	by 6/30
224	PG 1099	Thornycroft A2L-Challands Ross	B20F	New	6/29	1/31
239	PG 1757	Thornycroft BC-Challands Ross	B32R	New	7/29	1/31
238	PG 1758	Thornycroft BC-Challands Ross	B32R	New	7/29	1/31
175	PG 2018	Thornycroft A2L-Challands Ross	B20F	New	7/29	1/31
241	PG 3236	Thornycroft A2L-Challands Ross	B20F	New	10/29	1/31

242	PG 4226	Thornycroft A2L-Challands Ross	B20F	New	12/29	1/31
244	PG 9381	Tilling Stevens B10A2-Petty	B32R	New	5/30	1/31
245	PG 9382	Tilling Stevens B10A2-Petty	B32R	New	5/30	1/31
246	PG 9383	Tilling Stevens B10A2-Petty	B32R	New	5/30	1/31
247	PG 9384	Tilling Stevens B10A2-Petty	B32R	New	5/30	1/31
248	PG 9385	AJS Pilot-Petty	B26R	New	5/30	1/31

Note (A): Recorded by PSV Circle as new to Fox, but no mention in Woking Council licensing records. Guildford Council records suggest it was licensed to Locke, Guildford by late 1924.

Note (B): Only listed in Woking Council records September 1929–April 1930.

J. F. Hampton

Woking Council Licence No.	Registration No.	Chassis (& Body where known)	Body Configuration	Former Owner	Date In	Date Out
150	PB 8935	Napier	12	Stilwell, Sutton Green	5/22	2/24
154	PC 8947	Ford T	B14	New	7/22	3/29
150	PD 8586	Ford T	14	New	2/24	3/29
-	MD 9007	Caledon 4 ton	Ch		6/25	3/29
218	PD 7993	Ford T-Coulter	B14	Fox, St Johns	11/26	3/29

W. Hunt

Chertsey Council Licence No.	Registration No.	Chassis (& Body where known)	Body Configuration	Former Owner	Date In	Date Out
12	PB 6858		7	New(?)	by 2/22	/24

Hunt may have operated other vehicles.

V. Jenner

Woking Council Licence No.	Registration No.	Chassis (& Body where known)	Body Configuration	Former Owner	Date In	Date Out
6	CT 351	Brasier	8	Mills, St Johns	by 9/20	

H. T. Lintott

Guildford Council Licence No.	Registration No.	Chassis (& Body where known)	Body Configuration	Former Owner	Date In	Date Out
53	RO 9447	Chevrolet LO-Thurgood	B14	H Lintott, St Albans	4/28	/32
77	PK 3709	Chevrolet-Arnold & Comben(?)	B14	New	10/28	

	Registration No.	Chassis (& Body where known)	Body Configuration	Former Owner	Date In	Date Out
89	PG 254	Chevrolet LQ-Arnold Comben(?)	B14	New	5/29	11/37
-	RO 8804	Dodge-Strachan & Brown	B14	A Lintott, Petersfield	2/32	by 11/37
-	UR 4043	Chevrolet LQ	C14F	A Lintott, Petersfield	2/32	by /35
-	UR 4044	Chevrolet LQ	C14F	A Lintott, Petersfield	2/32	11/37
-	UR 4466	Guy OND	B20	A Lintott, Petersfield	2/32	11/37
-	UR 5780	Chevrolet LQ-Thurgood	B14	A Lintott, Petersfield	2/32	11/37
-	ACG 89	Bedford WLB-Thurgood	B20F	New	3/35	11/37
-	BOR 501	Dodge RBF-Reall	B26R	New	9/36	11/37

Vehicles shown as out 11/37 sold to S. Ansell. PG 254, UR 4044 and UR 4466 withdrawn and sold by Ansell by 3/38. UR 5780, ACG 89 and BOR 501 sold 6/38.

Vehicle purchased by S. Ansell:						
-	EXF 377	Dennis Pike-Dennis	C20F	New	3/38	6/38

A. T. Locke & Son

Guildford Council Licence No.	Registration No.	Chassis (& Body where known)	Body Configuration	Former Owner	Date In	Date Out
41	PD 3871	Ford Model T-Coulter	14	Fox, St Johns	c12/24	2/27
42	PD 4646		14	New	c12/24	11/27
51	PE 1800			New	2/25	
59	PE 6313	Ford Model T	C20	New	9/25	3/26

		Graham Bros	C20	(Body ex-PE 6313)		
59	PE 8539				3/26	
62	PE 9737			New	by 6/26	
68	PF 4135			New	9/26	
41	PF 9527	Guy	20	New	5/27	/36
44	PH 1172	Guy BB-United	B26D	New	6/27	by 2/36
66	PH 8431	Thornycroft-Arnold & Comben	B20D	New	4/28	
37	PK 1639	Abbott(?)	B20F	New	5/28	
42	PK 5639	Star Flyer VB4-Duple	B20F	New	2/29	
-	MT 1973	Star Flyer VB4-Duple	C20D	Webber,London N22	6/30	1/38
-	PL 3022	Dennis GL	B20F	New	10/30	by 4/36
-	PL 8827	Star Flyer VB4-Duple(?)	C24D	New	6/31	1/38
-	PJ 5970	Guy Victory ONDL-United	B20F	New	6/32	1/38
-	UR 4648	Guy Victory OND	B20F	Kirby,St Albans	4/33	by /35
-	APG 207	Guy Victory ONDL-United	C20F	New	6/33	1/38
-	CPA 875	Guy Wolf CFP-Beadle	B20F	New	1/35	1/38
-	CPE 222	Guy Wolf CFP-Beadle	B20F	New	3/35	1/38
-	CPH 130	Dennis Lancet-Dennis	C32C	New	5/35	1/38
-	DPD 858	Dennis Ace-Dennis	B20F	New	1/36	1/38
-	DPD 859	Dennis Ace-Dennis	B20F	New	1/36	1/38
-	EPK 29	Dennis Ace-Dennis	B20F	New	1/37	1/38
- (A)	EPL 628	Dennis Lancet II-Dennis	C32F	New	3/37	1/38

Note (A): Normal Control model.

B. H. Martin

Woking Council Licence No.	Registration No.	Chassis (& Body where known)	Body Configuration	Former Owner	Date In	Date Out
15 (A)	PD 6352	Ford		Settle, Horsell	12/27	(B)
42 (A)	PE 1419	Ford	14	Settle, Horsell	12/27	(B)
223	PH 2022	Guy	20	Settle, Horsell	12/27	3/31
237	VF 3002	Chevrolet LO-United	B14	United	c5/29	3/31
236	YV 9989				c5/29	/30

Note (A): Chertsey Council Licence No

Note (B): One of these two buses destroyed by fire 4/29.

F. W. Mills

Woking Council Licence No.	Registration No.	Chassis (& Body where known)	Body Configuration	Former Owner	Date In	Date Out
48	P 5413	(A)	O36R	New	by 1/12	
12	P 5585	Dennis	20	New	by 2/14	
-	PA 7175 (B)	Ford			by 9/15	
-	PA 7277	Ford	7		by 8/16	
12	CD 2597	Ford 20hp	4		by 10/17	
6	PA 7717	Ford			by 6/18	

Woking Council Licence No.	Registration No.	Chassis (& Body where known)	Body Configuration	Former Owner	Date In	Date Out
79	PA 7163	Singer (Ford?)			by 11/18	
22	PA 7174 (B)	Ford			by 11/18	.
111	BH 2927	Albion	10		by 1/19	
6	CT 351	Brasier			by 6/19	
48	PA 5546	Daimler	Ch		by 6/19	

Note (A): Original chassis of P 5413 unknown, but received new Dennis 35hp chassis in 1914.

Note (B): PA 7174 and PA 7175 may be the same vehicle (possible error in Council Minutes).

F. W. Renshaw & L. M. Leam

Woking Council Licence No.	Registration No.	Chassis (& Body where known)	Body Configuration	Former Owner	Date In	Date Out
74	PA 7746	Ford Model T		New	by 8/17	
116	PA 8365	Ford Model T		New	by 6/19	/25
-	P 8180	Ford Model T			11/22	by 5/24
184	PD 9889	Chevrolet	14	New	by 5/24	/25
201	PE 2415	Ford	14	New	4/25	by 6/27
213	PF 2824	Chevrolet	14	New	/25	
214	PE 8584	Chevrolet	14	New	2/26	
201	PF 5771	Chevrolet	14	New	/26	
228	PH 6898	Chevrolet 6W	20	New	2/28	
243	PG 5551	Dennis 30cwt-Strachan	B18F	New	1/30	5/39

Woking Council Licence No.	Registration No.	Chassis (& Body where known)	Body Configuration	Former Owner	Date In	Date Out
–	PJ 239	Bedford WLB	B20F	New	10/31	5/39
–	PJ 8068	Bedford WLB-Duple	B20F	New	9/32	5/39
–	APH 596	Bedford WLB-Duple	B20F	New	7/33	5/39

C. Ross

Woking Council Licence No.	Registration No.	Chassis (& Body where known)	Body Configuration	Former Owner	Date In	Date Out
165/225	PD 7273	Ford Model T	B14	New	by 9/23	1/28
167	PD 7721	Ford Model T	B14	New	by 9/23	1/28
206	PE 7147	Republic	B20	New	11/25	1/28
165	PF 9181	Morris 25/30cwt	B14	New	4/27	1/28

H. Settle

Woking Council Licence No.	Registration No.	Chassis (& Body where known)	Body Configuration	Former Owner	Date In	Date Out
	PC 5209		20	Burton, Maybury	9/23	by 9/24
15 (A)	PD 6352	Ford		New	by 9/24	12/27
42 (A)	PE 1419	Ford	14	New	by 6/25	12/27
223	PH 2022	Guy	20	New	4/27	12/27

Note (A): Chertsey Council Licence No.

A. C. Silk

Woking Council Licence No.	Registration No.	Chassis (& Body where known)	Body Configuration	Former Owner	Date In	Date Out
	BH 2927	Albion	10	Bullman, St Johns	by 11/23	/24

A. G. Smith

Woking Council Licence No.	Registration No.	Chassis (& Body where known)	Body Configuration	Former Owner	Date In	Date Out
141	PC 5710	Ford Model T	14	New	10/21	1/23
143		Ford Model T			by 5/22	1/23
149	PC 7324	Ford Model T	Ch20	New	by 5/22	
156	PC 9724	Ford Model T	14	New	1/23	
157	PC 9725	Ford Model T	14	New	1/23	10/25
187	PD 2642	Overland	14	New	/23	6/26
164	PD 6642	Ford Model T		New	by 6/23	10/25
168	PD 8017	GMC	16	New	12/23	10/25
183	PD 1174	Fiat-Coulter	C20	New	by 5/24	10/25
204	PE 6848	Republic-Coulter	B20F	New	10/25	6/26
205	PE 7415	Republic-Coulter	B20F	New	11/25	6/26

S. Spooner

Woking Council Licence No.	Registration No.	Chassis (& Body where known)	Body Configuration	Former Owner	Date In	Date Out
190	PD 3733	(A)	14	New	11/24	
194	PE 1000	(A)	14	New	2/25	
	LM 7462	[Taxi]			by 9/26	10/26

Note (A): At least one of these buses was an Overland, destroyed by fire 9/26.

A. H. Stilwell

Guildford Council Licence No.	Registration No.	Chassis (& Body where known)	Body Configuration	Former Owner	Date In	Date Out
	PB 8935	Napier	12	New (?)	7/21	5/22
22	PB 6848				5/22	7/26

S. Tanner

Woking Council Licence No.	Registration No.	Chassis (& Body where known)	Body Configuration	Former Owner	Date In	Date Out
			Ch14		by 7/21	
195/215	PC 9313	Dennis	Ch24	New	7/22	9/31
199/195	PE 2077	Dennis 50cwt-Strachan & Brown	B20F	New	4/25	10/28

	Registration No.	Chassis (& Body where known)	Body Configuration	Former Owner	Date In	Date Out
199	PE 9850	Dennis 30cwt	B18F	New	3/26	10/28
219	PF 5831	Dennis 30cwt-Strachan & Brown	B19F	New	12/26	10/28
216	PF 7274	Dennis 30cwt	B19F	New	1/27	by 10/28

H. E. Trigg

Guildford Council Licence No.	Registration No.	Chassis (& Body where known)	Body Configuration	Former Owner	Date In	Date Out
40	PD 3376		14	New	10/24	by 12/25
46	PE 1032			New	2/25	2/26

Woking Autocar

Woking Council Licence No.	Registration No.	Chassis (& Body where known)	Body Configuration	Former Owner	Date In	Date Out
	AB 3523	Ford	12	New (?)	by 8/17	
76	PA 7553	Ford		New	by 6/18	8/19

The Aldershot & District Traction Co., Ltd.

NOTICE.

Guildford, Chobham, Ascot, and Windsor

On and after **FRIDAY, MARCH 23rd, 1928,** a Service of Omnibuses will operate between **GUILDFORD** and **WINDSOR** as under, until further Notice : —

SERVICE 51.   WEEK-DAYS & SUNDAYS.

		a m N.S.	a m	p m N.S.	p m	p m	p m	p m
Guildford Technical Institute	dep.	8 15	1025	12 0	2 25	4 25	6 25	8 25
Stoughton, Royal Hotel	,,	8 25	1035	1210	2 35	4 35	6 35	8 35
Worplesdon, New Inn	,,	8 35	1045	1220	2 46	4 46	6 46	8 46
Pirbright, Fox Inn	,,	8 39	1049	1224	2 50	4 50	6 50	8 50
Worplesdon, Golf Club Turning	,,	8 44	1054	1229	2 55	4 55	6 55	8 55
Knaphill, Garibaldi	,,	8 48	1058	1233	2 59	4 59	6 59	8 59
Chobham Church	,,	8 58	11 8	1243	3 9	5 9	7 9	9 9
Sunningdale Station	,,	9 11	1121	1256	3 22	5 22	7 22	9 22
Sunninghill Post Office	,,	9 18	1128	1 3	3 29	5 29	7 29	9 29
Ascot, Horse and Groom	,,	9 26	1136	1 11	3 37	5 37	7 37	9 37
Ascot Heath Cross Roads	,,	9 31	1141	1 16	3 42	5 42	7 42	9 42
Brookside (Hatchet Lane Farm)	,,	9 33	1143	1 18	3 44	5 44	7 44	9 44
Lovel Hill, Fleur de Lys	,,	9 35	1145	1 20	3 46	5 46	7 46	9 46
Winkfield, Squirrel Hotel	,,	9 41	1151	1 26	3 52	5 52	7 52	9 52
Clewer Green, Prince Albert	,,	9 50	12 0	1 35	4 1	6 1	8 1	10 1
Windsor Castle	arr.	9 59	12 9	1 44	4 10	6 10	8 10	1010

		a m N.S.	a m N.S.	p m	p m	p m	p m	p m
Windsor Castle	dep.	8 30	1015	1215	2 15	4 30	6 15	8 30
Clewer Green, Prince Albert	,,	8 39	1024	1224	2 24	4 39	6 24	8 39
Winkfield, Squirrel Hotel	,,	8 48	1033	1233	2 33	4 48	6 33	8 48
Lovel Hill, Fleur de Lys	,,	8 54	1039	1239	2 39	4 54	6 39	8 54
Brookside (Hatchet Lane Farm)	,,	8 56	1041	1241	2 41	4 56	6 41	8 56
Ascot Heath Cross Roads	,,	8 58	1043	1243	2 43	4 58	6 43	8 58
Ascot, Horse and Groom	,,	9 3	1048	1248	2 48	5 3	6 48	9 3
Sunninghill Post Office	,,	9 11	1056	1256	2 56	5 11	6 56	9 11
Sunningdale Station	,,	9 18	11 3	1 3	3 3	5 18	7 3	9 18
Chobham Church	,,	9 31	1116	1 16	3 16	5 31	7 16	9 31
Knaphill, Garibaldi	,,	9 41	1126	1 26	3 26	5 41	7 26	9 41
Worplesdon, Golf Club Turning	,,	9 45	1130	1 30	3 30	5 45	7 30	9 45
Pirbright, Fox Inn	,,	9 50	1135	1 35	3 35	5 50	7 35	9 50
Worplesdon, New Inn	,,	9 54	1139	1 39	3 39	5 54	7 39	9 54
Stoughton, Royal Hotel	,,	10 4	1149	1 49	3 49	6 4	7 49	10 4
Guildford Technical Institute	arr.	1014	1159	1 59	3 59	6 14	7 59	1014

N.S. Not on Sundays.

This Time Table is issued subject to the Conditions and Regulations as printed in the Company's Time Tables and in Notices issued from time to time.

Halimote Road,
    Aldershot,
March 14th, 1928.

By Order,
N. GRAY,
Traffic Superintendent.

Clement & Son, Printers, 99, Victoria Road, Aldershot. 20992.

The Aldershot & District Traction Co., Ltd.

NOTICE.

Woking, Knaphill & Bagshot Service

On and after SATURDAY, 13th OCTOBER, 1928, an Improved Service of Omnibuses
will operate between

WOKING, KNAPHILL, WEST END, LIGHTWATER & BAGSHOT,

as under, until further notice.

Services 4, 34, 34a & 34b. WEEK-DAYS & SUNDAYS

		a m	a m	a m	a m	a m	a m	a m	u m	a m	m p m	p m	p m	p m	p m		p m	p m
Woking Station	dep.	7 30	7 50	8 30	8 50	9 30	9 50	10 30	10 50	11 30	12 30	1 30	1 50	2 30	2 50		9 50	10 30
St. John's Post Office	"	7 38	7 58	8 38	8 58	9 38	9 58	10 38	10 58	11 38	12 38	1 38	1 58	2 38	2 58		9 58	10 38
Knaphill, Garibaldi	arr.	7 47	8 8	8 47	9 9	9 47	10 8	10 47	11 8	11 47	12 8	1 47	2 8	2 47			10 8	10 48
Knaphill, Garibaldi	dep.	7 48	8 10	8 48	9 10	9 48	10 10	10 48	11*10	11 48	12*10	1 48	2 10	2 48			10 10	..
Bisley Post Office	"	7 51	8 13	8 51	9 13	9 51	10 13	10 51	11*13	11 51	12 13	1 51	2 13	2 51			10 13	..
Bisley, Hen & Chicken	"	7 53	8 15	8 53	9 15	9 53	10 15	10 53	11*15	11 53	12*15	1 53	2 15	2 53			10 15	..
Westend, Wheatsheaf	"	7 58	8 18	8 58	9 18	9 58	10 18	10 58	11*18	11 58	12*18	1 58	2 18	2 58			10 18	..
Lightwater War Memorial	"	8 3	8 23	9 3	9 23	10 3	10 23	11 3	11*23	12 3	12*23	2 3	2 23	3 3			10 23	..
Bagshot Square	arr.	8 8	8 28	9 8	9 28	10 8	10 28	11 8	11*28	12 8	12*28	2 8	2 28	3 8			10 28	..

		a m	a m	a m	a m	a m	a m	a m	a m	a m	m p m	p m	p m	p m	p m		p m	p m
Bagshot Square	dep.	7 30	8 30	8 50	9 30	9 50	10 30	10 50	11 30	11 50	12 30	12 50	1 30	1 50	2 30	2 50	9 30	9 50	10 30
Lightwater War Memorial	"	7 35	8 35	8 55	9 35	9 55	10 35	10 55	11 35	11 55	12 35	12 55	1 35	1 55	2 35	2 55	9 35	9 55	10 35
Westend Wheatsheaf	"	7 40	8 40	9 0	9 40	9 59	10 40	10 59	11 40	11 59	12 40	12 59	1 40	1 59	2 40	2 59	9 40	9 59	10 40
Bisley, Hen & Chicken	"	7 45	8 45	9 3	9 45	10 3	10 45	11 3	11 45	12 3	12 45	3 1	1 45	3 2	2 45	3	9 45	10 3	10 45
Bisley Post Office	"	7 47	8 47	9 5	9 47	10 5	10 47	11 5	11 47	12 5	12 47	1	1 47	2 5	2 47	3 5	9 47	10 5	10 47
Knaphill, Garibaldi	arr.	7 49	8 49	9 7	9 49	10 7	10 49	11 7	11 49	12 7	12 49	1	1 49	2 7	2 49	3 7	9 49	10 7	10 49
Knaphill, Garibaldi	dep.	7 50	8 50	9 10	9 50	10 10	10 50	11 10	11 50	12*10	12 50	1†	1 50	2 10	2 50	3 10	9 50	..	..
St. John's Post Office	"	8 0	9 0	9 20	10 0	10 20	11 0	11 20	12 0	12†20	1 0	1†	2 0	2 20	3 0	3 10	10 0	..	..
Woking Station	arr.	8 8	9 8	9 28	10 8	10 28	11 8	11 28	12 8	12†28	1 8	1†	2 8	2 28	3 8	3 28	10 8	..	..

* NOT SUNDAYS. † Starts from KNAPHILL SUNDAYS.

§ This Omnibus will wait for the conclusion of the last performance of the Woking Cinema and
run to KNAPHILL on MONDAYS, TUESDAYS and THURSDAYS, and will be extended to BROOKWOOD,
PIRBRIGHT and BLACKDOWN on WEDNESDAYS, FRIDAYS and SATURDAYS.

This Time Table is issued subject to the Conditions and Regulations as printed in the Company's Time Tables
and in notices issued from time to time.

Head Office, Aldershot.
10th October, 1928.

By Order, N. GRAY,
Traffic Superintendent.

Clement & Son, Printers, 99, Victoria Road, Aldershot. 21678.

The Aldershot & District Traction Co., Ltd.

NOTICE.

Woking, Maybury, Send & Guildford.

On and after **Wednesday, July 17th, 1929**, the **Woking—Maybury Service**
will be Revised and certain Journeys extended to **Guildford**, to run as under, until further Notice:

SERVICES 47 & 47a. WEEK-DAYS

		a m									p m											
Woking Station	dep.	7 30	7 45	8 0	8 30	9 0	9 30	10 0	10 30	11 0	11 30	12 0	12 30	1 0	1 30	2 0	2 30	3 0	3 30	4 0	4 30	5 0	5 30	6 0
Maybury Inn	"	7 40	7 55	8 10	8 40	9 10	9 40	10 10	10 40	11 10	11 40	12 10	12 40	1 10	1 40	2 10	2 40	3 10	3 40	4 10	4 40	5 10	5 40	6 10
Old Woking Post Office	"	7 46	..	8 46	..	9 46	..	10 46	..	11 46	..	12 46	..	1 46	..	2 46	..	3 46	..	4 46	..	5 46	..
Send, New Inn	"	7 49	..	8 49	..	9 49	..	10 49	..	11 49	..	12 49	..	1 49	..	2 49	..	3 49	..	4 49	..	5 49	..
Burpham, Green Man	"	8 2	..	9 2	..	10 2	..	11 2	..	12 2	..	1 2	..	2 2	..	3 2	..	4 2	..	5 2	..	6 2	..
Guildford, Technical Institute	arr.	8 15	..	9 15	..	10 15	..	11 15	..	12 15	..	1 15	..	2 15	..	3 15	..	4 15	..	5 15	..	6 15	..

WEEK-DAYS—continued. SUNDAYS.

		a m					a m	p m												
Woking Station	dep.	6 30	7 0	7 30	8 0	8 30	9 0	9 30	10 25	12 45	1 15	2 15	2 45	3 15	4 0	4 55	5	6	7 0	7 30	8 0	9 15	10 0
Maybury Inn	"	6 40	7 10	7 40	8 10	8 40	9 10	9 40	10 35	12 55	1 25	2 25	2 55	3 25	4 10	5 5	5	6	7 10	7 40	8 10	9 25	10 10
Old Woking Post Office	"	6 46	..	7 46	..	8 46	..	9 46	..	..	..	..	..	..	..	..	..	..	..	..
Send, New Inn	"	6 49	..	7 49	..	8 49	..	9 49	..	..	..	..	..	..	..	..	..	..	..	..
Burpham, Green Man	"	7 2	..	8 2	..	9 2	..	10 2	..	..	..	..	..	..	..	..	..	..	..	..
Guildford, Technical Institute	arr.	7 15	..	8 15	..	9 15	..	10 15	..	..	..	..	..	..	..	..	..	..	..	..

WEEK-DAYS.

		a m					p m												
Guildford, Technical Institute	dep.	..	8 40	..	9 40	..	10 40	..	11 40	..	12 40	..	1 40	..	2 40	..	3 40	..	4 40	..	5 40	..	6 40
Burpham, Green Man	"	..	8 53	..	9 53	..	10 53	..	11 53	..	12 53	..	1 53	..	2 53	..	3 53	..	4 53	..	5 53	..	6 53
Send, New Inn	"	..	9 6	..	10 6	..	11 6	..	12 6	..	1 6	..	2 6	..	3 6	..	4 6	..	5 6	..	6 6	..	7 6
Old Woking Post Office	"	..	9 9	..	10 9	..	11 9	..	12 9	..	1 9	..	2 9	..	3 9	..	4 9	..	5 9	..	6 9	..	7 9
Maybury Inn	"	8 15	8 45	9 15	9 45	10 15	10 45	11 15	11 45	12 15	12 45	1 15	1 45	2 15	2 45	3 15	3 45	4 15	4 45	5 15	5 45	6 15	6 45	7 15
Woking Station	arr.	8 25	8 55	9 25	9 55	10 25	10 55	11 25	11 55	12 25	12 55	1 25	1 55	2 25	2 55	3 25	3 55	4 25	4 55	5 25	5 55	6 25	6 55	7 25

WEEK-DAYS—continued. SUNDAYS.

		p m				a m	p m												
Guildford, Technical Institute	dep.	..	7 40	..	8 40	..	9 40	10 20		a m	p m										
Burpham, Green Man	"	..	7 53	..	8 53	..	9 53	10 33		..	..	..	..	..	..	..	..	..
Send, New Inn	"	..	8 6	..	9 6	..	10 6	10 46		..	..	..	..	..	..	..	..	..
Old Woking Post Office	"	..	8 9	..	9 9	..	10 9	10 49		..	..	..	..	..	..	..	..	..
Maybury Inn	"	7 45	8 15	8 45	9 15	9 45	10 15	10 55		10 40	1 0	1 55	2 30	3 0	3 30	4 0	4 30	5 0	3 35	6 30	7 15	7 45	8 35	9 35	10 10
Woking Station	arr.	7 55	8 25	8 55	9 25	9 55	10 25	11 5		10 50	1 10	2 5	2 40	3 10	3 40	4 0	4 35	5 10	4 56	4 07	2 57	5 58	4 59	4 5	10 20

A late Omnibus will leave Woking Plaza Cinema at conclusion of last Performance every Week-day for Maybury Inn and return to Woking.

This Time Table is issued subject to the Conditions and Regulations as printed in the Company's Official Time Tables, and in Notices issued
from time to time.

Head Office: Halimote Road, Aldershot.
June 14th, 1929.

By Order, N. GRAY,
Traffic Superintendent.

Clement & Son, Printers, 99, Victoria Road, Aldershot—22541.